the Pastry Queen Christmas

the Pastry Queen Christmas

Rebecca Rather
with alison oresman

PHOTOGRAPHY BY
Laurie Smith

Big-Hearted Holiday Entertaining, Texas Style

TEN SPEED PRESS
Berkeley | Toronto

Ten Speed Press
PO Box 7123
Berkeley, California 94707
www.tenspeed.com

Distributed in Australia by Simon and
Schuster Australia, in Canada by Ten Speed
Press Canada, in New Zealand by Southern
Publishers Group, in South Africa by Real
Books, and in the United Kingdom and Europe
by Publishers Group UK.

Jacket and text design by Toni Tajima
Photography by Laurie Smith
Food styling by Erica McNeish
Prop styling by Samantha Robinson
Makeup by Amy Oresman

Library of Congress Cataloging-in-Publication
Data

Rather, Rebecca.
    The pastry queen Christmas: big-hearted holi-
day entertaining, Texas style/Rebecca Rather with
Alison Oresman; photography by Laurie Smith.
        p. cm.
    Summary: "Ninety-five holiday recipes from
Rebecca Rather's Rather Sweet Bakery and Café,
plus Christmas craft and entertaining ideas
inspired by the traditions of small-town America"—Provided by publisher.
    Includes index.
    ISBN 978-1-58008-790-2
    1. Christmas cookery. 2. Entertaining.
3. Rather Sweet Bakery and Café. I. Oresman,
Alison. II. Title.
    TX739.2.C45R38 2007
    641.5'686—dc22
                        2007012439

Printed in China

3 4 5 6 7 8 9 10 — 11 10 09 08

With love to my daughter, Frances:
These recipes are for you. You are my
Christmas; you are my everything.

—R. R.

To Warren, Danny, and Callie for your
unwavering love and support.

—A. O.

Contents

Acknowledgments

WRITING A BOOK IS a community effort, and happily for me, I live and work in an extraordinary community.

Thank you to the town of Fredericksburg and all of my great customers, who have supported me and acted as willing and cheerful subjects as I tested recipes for my first book and now the second. No one complained once—even when I served Cajun Roast Turkey and Corn Bread Dressing as a lunch special during the dog days of August.

I especially treasure the kids who frequent the bakery, peeking in to say hi as I'm working in the kitchen, and the parents who regularly make that possible. My young friends bring an energy and light that sustains me every day.

My business partner, Dan Kamp, keeps the bakery running smoothly, even while making endless emergency runs to the local HEB supermarket for a few last-minute ingredients I suddenly need to test yet another recipe. The publishing of my first book meant more days away from the bakery to teach classes throughout Texas, as well as embarking on a summer-long book tour. I left with confidence, knowing my able kitchen staff had it all under control. Thanks to Rosa Albiter Espinoza, Marcela Albiter, Romelia Arias, Blanca Aguirre, Beatriz and Tomas Albiter, and Bertine Jaramillo. Thanks also to my wonderful wait staff.

Some of my best friends are some of our best customers, which means I get to see them most days. I am so grateful to have them all in my life. Jackie Currie is often on hand, and she's never shy about sharing her astute assessments on how things ought to be run. (We don't always heed her advice; she might get a swelled head.) Lane Hutchins comes by for lunch several times a week and brings me minute-by-minute bulletins concerning my beloved horse, Junior, who boards with her. (I especially appreciate it when I get busy and can't escape from my kitchen to see him as much as I'd like.)

Orthopedic surgeon Dan Robertson expertly put me back together when I shattered my wrist during the final stages of writing this book, and his wife, Kim, lovingly nursed me back to health after the surgery. After my wrist injury, kitchen whiz Sam McNeely moved back to town just in time to become my literal right-hand woman. She spent countless evenings helping me test the book's last sixteen recipes.

Thank goodness for Penny Hughes, who runs Der Küchen Laden, one of Texas's best kitchen stores, located just across the street. Whenever I need a cooking implement, she's got it. Thanks to Lauren Bade, a wonderful friend and supporter, who gussies up my photo shoots by lending me beautiful accessories from her eponymous gift shop.

Doug Comstock and his boys helped me in too many ways to count, and Paige Conn tested recipes once again and provided her usual excellent suggestions. I also want to thank her fifth-grade art class from Fredericksburg Elementary for making one of the most beautiful and original Christmas trees ever (see page 131). Inspired by artist Wayne Thiebaud, the students decorated it with colorful papier-mâché cupcakes, cake slices, and cookies and topped it with a bright red cherry. The sign on the tree read: "Merry Christmas with a Cherry on Top." I bought the tree at a local charity auction this year and displayed it at the bakery, where it drew countless admiring glances. I'm sure it will become a Christmas tradition here for years to come. Thanks to everyone, family and friends alike, for offering their favorite recipes for this book.

None of this would have been possible without the folks at Ten Speed Press: publisher Lorena Jones, for continuing to believe; editors Lily Binns and Julie Bennett; and Dennis Hayes, a steadfast friend. Ten Speed art director Toni Tajima has given the book a distinctive and beautiful look. Thanks to super agent Doe Coover, who handles all situations with her customary cool and common sense.

Talented food photographer Laurie Smith, together with the endlessly creative food stylist Erica McNeish and prop stylist Sam Robinson, helped to make me and my food look good. (The former is a little harder than the latter, but Los Angeles makeup artist Amy Oresman used her considerable skills to aid me in the looking-good department.) Laurie, Erica, and Sam join me in thanking Kathy Harrison for the use of her chic guest house.

A special thanks to Lady Bird Johnson and her family for allowing us to visit and photograph the LBJ Ranch in Stonewall, and to Sue Bellows, the Johnson family's personal chef, for sharing several of her holiday recipes.

I am indebted to Jay and Patty Jones for graciously opening their home and property for our Ranch Barn Brunch party and for hosting the event with their characteristic grace, good humor, and charm.

Thanks to Alison Oresman, my cowriter, friend, and confidante. And finally, I'm grateful for the chance to write this book, which taught me something new about the spirit of Christmas and helped me uncover a deeper meaning in the holidays and a greater appreciation for my friends and family and the love they bring into the world.

—R. R.

WRITING CAN BE a lonely process. It helps to collaborate, and it is my good fortune to have found a most satisfying and excellent collaborator in my friend the talented chef Rebecca Rather. Who would have thought that our mutual interest in horses would have led to a successful partnership as coauthors? (We met on horseback at a culinary professionals' conference and decided to join forces to create a book.) Rebecca and I were neophytes when we embarked on our first project, but we've grown and learned together. Our latest effort took a lot less time and was a lot more fun. I'm confident the trend will continue. Thanks for everything, Rebecca.

Plenty of others contributed to this book, first and foremost photographer Laurie Smith, whose luscious photos, dedication to her craft, and unshakable optimism make working with her a continuing joy. Food stylist Erica McNeish works her transformative magic on all that is around her—from the food to the location—and keeps us laughing along the way. She and prop stylist Sam Robinson make a formidable team. (A special thanks to Erica for her technical help on the gingerbread project.) Los Angeles makeup artist Amy Oresman flew in to make everyone look gorgeous for the photo shoot and flew home having acquired a new group of friends and admirers.

I'm grateful to all of my friends in the Pacific Northwest. My Hilltop neighbors are my most enthusiastic taste testers, and I value their opinions greatly. Emily Anderson continues to pepper me with valuable, no-nonsense advice, and Kristen Webb provides invaluable assistance with recipe testing. Marcia Houdek-Jimenez's expert guidance ensures that I stay on track. My yoga teacher, Kathleen Hunt, along with my yogini classmates, keeps me grounded throughout the writing process, and my work with Colleen Willoughby and the Washington Women's Foundation feeds and sustains my soul—necessary nourishment for any writer.

Thanks to my father, Donald Oresman, once involved in the publishing business himself, for his probing questions and unflagging interest in my writing projects. Once again, my mother, Pat Oresman, came to the rescue and flew from her New York home to spend a week helping to test recipes in my Bellevue, Washington, kitchen. (Every morning at 7 A.M. my adorable eighty-two-year-old mom stationed herself in the kitchen, ready for duty.)

Finally, a heartfelt thanks to my husband and children, who surround me with the love and support I need to be productive. Thanks especially to my son, Danny, who edited every page of the raw manuscript with tremendous precision and insight. I had a hunch he might have a knack for editing, but his ability surpassed my expectations.

My daughter, Callie, helped keep my spirits high with her constant encouragement. My husband, Warren, provided me with invaluable technical help with the gingerbread house directions and templates (thank goodness for his mastery of geometry). Once again, he helps to make me look (and feel) good.

—A. O.

Introduction

PRACTICALLY THE WHOLE TOWN turns out for the annual nighttime Christmas Parade on Main Street, the official start of Fredericksburg's holiday season. Townspeople even park their vehicles (mostly beefy pick-ups) on the diagonal the night before to ensure a good view. Come parade night, their legs dangle from open tailgates as they watch the floats go by. Folks who failed to park early throng the sidewalks and squeeze between the trucks, some perched on hay bales, others on collapsible chairs.

If you're a local and you're not watching the parade, you're probably participating in it. The Fredericksburg High School Marching Band, tubas sparkling with Christmas lights, strides down Main Street, made extra wide in the nineteenth century to accommodate horse-drawn buggies; local churches create floats reenacting biblical scenes; the undefeated Heritage High School football team glides by in full uniform; the red-robed Peach Queen from nearby Stonewall waves, as does Miss Comfort, Texas (another neighboring town), and her court, all decked out in mini-skirts and cowboy boots. Don Jackson, from the Texas Longhorn Ranch in Stonewall, rides on the back of his enormous "reinsteer," really a Texas longhorn range steer with Christmas lights twisted through its extraordinarily large rack. The steer, named Bevo in honor of the University of Texas mascot, was an unwilling participant this year, forcing Don to dismount and push the reluctant animal from behind.

Girl Scouts, the nation's first Head Start Program in Stonewall, the local pioneer museum, the Fredericksburg Society for the Prevention of Cruelty to Animals, and the used-farm-implement dealer are among those parading down the street, which is bright with a galaxy of white Christmas lights. One year, Santa rode through on a red jeep at the parade's end, high-fiving kids along the parade route. This year, he led the parade in a sleigh. For the unlucky few who don't make it to the event in person, two competing local radio stations broadcast it live.

I cried the first time I saw this parade. In 2000, I'd just moved from Austin to open a new bakery, and I suppose the parade symbolized everything I valued about living in a small town. I never would have guessed that

1

the following year I'd be in the parade myself, on horseback. It's overwhelming, turning the corner onto Main Street, with the Christmas lights blazing and the spectators cheering and clapping.

I did not anticipate the warm reception my business partner, Dan Kamp, and I would receive when we opened the Rather Sweet Bakery and Café seven years ago. Many of our current regulars—most have become good friends—came in from the start, and all were ready to lend a hand. Early on, customer Kim Robertson noticed we were short on dish towels, so she rushed out to the local discount store and returned with an armload. Now she's one of my best friends, stopping by for a kitchen visit most days.

Not that the beginning was easy. Dan waited tables, washed dishes, took care of the front of the house, and did the books, while I got up at 5 A.M. to start the day's baking. Then I worked throughout the day to keep the bakery case full and to fix lunch for a growing number of customers. We had zero help and were at the bakery thirty-four hours a day.

Gradually, we hired a kitchen staff and dishwasher. Within a few years, business expanded and so did the bakery. We leased the upstairs (formerly a clothing store) and went from twenty-five to sixty-four indoor seats. Jackie Currie, a regular with a fabulous sense of style, helped me decorate the upstairs dining room. She even took me to Mexico to buy authentic tin sconces, artwork, and other decorative pieces that transformed the second-floor dining room into a warm yet classy space. Jackie calls the bakery kitchen "my

kitchen away from home," and asks: "Where else can you be in a restaurant kitchen just hanging out?" Jackie, who has never called me anything but "Baker," holds court at her regular table in the first-floor dining room almost every day. She's not shy about giving us advice. Lately, she's been pushing for cloth napkins, but Dan says he has to draw the line somewhere: "You are dreaming there," he tells her.

My career as a pastry chef began well before I came to Fredericksburg. I started in catering and went on to become executive pastry chef for Tony Vallone, one of Houston's most celebrated restaurateurs. (Recently, he hired me to return as a consultant.) Next, I worked as an executive chef in charge of developing a new line of desserts for a national chain. Finally, I opened my own bakery in Austin. Still, I can't help feeling that I've come of age during my time in Fredericksburg. The bakery/café has survived for more than seven years, quite a feat considering the small percentage of restaurants that make it to a second year. A host of national food magazines have carried stories about the bakery and also included my recipes in their pages. I wrote my first book, *The Pastry Queen,* and to my great excitement and surprise, it sold very well. Some days, it's hard to get much done in the kitchen for all the interruptions from tourists asking me to autograph their newly purchased copies. Just recently, Rather Sweet Bakery and Café was named one of the top ten bakeries in the nation by renowned pastry chef Nick Malgieri in *USA Today.* Not bad for a self-taught baker who was once so broke she had to trade desserts for haircuts.

All of this attention could lead to a swelled head, but not in Fredericksburg. My staff and my regulars (sometimes it's hard to tell the difference) keep me in line. It's hard to take yourself too seriously when customers act as though they own the place. I am constantly interrupted in the kitchen. They enter at will directly from the back door, and get their kicks by cracking jokes at my expense. How many big-time pastry chefs do you know who get repeated calls from eight-year-olds requesting cookie-baking play dates? I just scheduled one with my friend Caroline Elizabeth to make and decorate Christmas cookies. No doubt we'll be baking at least a few of my signature Christmas pigs with red and green scarves. (See page 133 for other ideas.)

Then there is Redding S. Sugg, Jr., a lovely older gentleman who accompanies his wife to the bakery several times a week. He politely but repeatedly requested that I make a chicken gumbo for an occasional lunch special and even sent me a recipe he remembered from childhood. He says, "My recollection extends to the period when the recipe might have begun matter-of-factly with 'First catch your chicken'—in which event you had head, neck, back, feet, and perhaps wings, and the soup was an economy dish making use of the bony parts." When I finished developing Day-after-Christmas Cajun Turkey Gumbo for this book (page 158), I made sure he and his wife got a hot, steaming bowl. He wrote me a second letter telling me how much he enjoyed the soup. I was thrilled until I read the next line, saying it wasn't quite as good as his mother's. He suggested it could use a touch more tomato and okra.

I admit to being a bit of a Scrooge before moving to Fredericksburg. Holidays for chefs are always the busiest and most stressful times. It starts with Halloween, gets even crazier at

Thanksgiving, and then there's Christmas and catering for holiday parties. I work just as hard here as ever, but it's close to impossible not to get swept up in the Christmas spirit when it is all around you. How grumpy can one be after witnessing the annual Santa Run down Main Street, when several dozen townspeople put on makeshift Santa costumes and race for charity? This year, one contestant put on red flannel pajamas with an open flap in the back that exposed a fake bottom. Last year, to preserve an authentic Santa look, only runners in boots could qualify. Complaints about the resulting blisters convinced organizers to allow tennis shoes for this year's run. What we have here is the epitome of small-town Texas, and for me, it's hard to resist.

The downside, of course, is everyone gets into everyone else's business. Ever since I began work on this book, friends have been

3

plying me with their favorite family Christmas recipes, hoping they will make it into the book. Many are here. To me, the holidays mean friends and family, and I've shared so many delicious holiday meals with people I love that I am delighted to include them. Other recipes came from family members, many of whom are no longer with us. My grandmother died when I was a young girl before I got to know her well, but cooking her Mustard-Baked Ham (page 19) somehow makes me feel closer to her. The spirit of my mother, who passed away when I was twenty-one, is always with me at Christmas, when we celebrate the holiday with a feast that includes her old-fashioned corn bread dressing (page 156). Looking through her old handwritten recipes brings me back to the days when we cooked side by side in our colorful Mexican-tiled kitchen. I'm so thankful that this book will provide my daughter, Frances, with family recipes that might otherwise have been lost.

The Pastry Queen Christmas offers a variety of recipes that fit into various party themes, such as Ranch Barn Brunch, Christmas Eve, and Outdoor Tree Trimming. The themes are just ideas, not to be taken literally. Be sure to mix and match recipes from varying chapters to create your own custom-made holiday event. Nor do I mean to suggest that you hold a Holiday Open House by cooking all fifteen recipes. Pick the recipes that appeal to you and don't worry about the rest.

Writing this book has knocked any vestiges of grinchiness out of me and put me in touch with the pure joy of cooking great food with and for those I love during the holiday season. In fact, I'll be adding several new recipes to the Christmas-dinner repertoire when I return to my childhood home this Christmas (Margie's Christmas Squash, page 161, and Sticky Toffee Pudding with Brandy Butterscotch Sauce, page 118).

I hope you'll do the same.

—Rebecca Rather

CHAPTER ONE

HOLIDAY OPEN HOUSE

THE ANNUAL CHRISTMAS PARADE in early December signals the beginning of the holiday party season in Fredericksburg. Long before that, local hostesses and businesses begin calling to inquire about catering. Last season, I provided desserts for a party in a magnificent home with breathtaking views of the night sky and the valley below. (City lights that dim the starlit sky are foreign to us here.) I put together several platters of mini Key lime pies, a bakery favorite included in this chapter. (At the bakery, and in the recipe on page 35, the pie is king-sized, making it much faster to produce than the bite-sized versions.)

When customers ask for advice about giving holiday parties, an open house is always my first suggestion. Casual by definition, open houses work for groups of all sizes and ages. Serving the food buffet style frees you to move around and mingle with guests. Careful advance planning and do-ahead recipes are your keys to success. Many of the recipes in this chapter can be made at least one day before serving. (My Creamy Chicken Lasagna on page 24 can be made the day before and baked just before serving, and

just about every dessert in this chapter can be made early.) When planning your menu, try to balance make-ahead recipes with those that need fixing the day of the party.

When testing and developing recipes for this book, my coauthor and I shared a running joke involving a fictional Aunt Susie. On particularly grueling days, after testing numerous recipes with many left to go, I'd say, "Just get Aunt Susie to do it." We'd crack up and soldier on. There was a kernel of wisdom in our jest. You may or may not have an Aunt Susie, but enlisting family and friends to help with preparty cooking is an ingenious way to make party prep as much fun as the event itself. Plan the menu, buy all of the groceries necessary, have all of your recipes on hand, and invite a couple of friends over to help. Some of my most rewarding conversations have taken place over the kitchen counter. This approach could even work with your teenage children, although you may have to offer financial incentives.

One of the best things about Christmas in Fredericksburg is that everyone seems to get into the holiday mood, including Beau, the bakery dog (above). It helps that we have our own little spirit of Christmas, Rosemary Estenson. The owner of the Fredericksburg Brewery next door to my Rather Sweet Bakery and Café, she's one of the town's chief Christmas organizers/enforcers. If Main Street merchants don't have their Christmas decorations up in time for the Christmas parade, they hear about it. This year, Rosemary paid a visit to Root, a clothing store on Main Street, to suggest that the window decorations needed beefing up. Owner Castle Heep complied and was glad she did. Her store looked extra festive for an open house held the night of the parade, and the place was packed.

Old-Fashioned Eggnog

Classic eggnog is not easy to make, but it is sure to dazzle your holiday guests. This version is cooked, to kill any bacteria in the eggs. And it can be made mostly in advance and refrigerated for up to 3 days. Just before the guests arrive, whip the cream, fold it into the eggnog, and serve with a sprinkle of fresh nutmeg. One taste of this, and you'll happily give up grocery-store eggnog for good. Lucky for me, I don't have to go farther than my backyard henhouse for fresh eggs. I have Silkies, Rhode Island Reds, and Araucanas and I've named each hen after a first lady. (Unfortunately, Nancy Reagan ran off a while back, never to be seen again.) Each breed produces a characteristic egg. My favorites are the light blue-green Araucana eggs. Aside from standard chicken feed, my brood gets to feast on leftover bakery products, which I suspect gives their eggs a special Rather Sweet flavor.

{ Yield: Six 1-cup servings }

3½ cups heavy cream

6 large eggs

1½ cups sugar

Pinch of kosher salt

¼ cup Myers's dark rum

½ cup whiskey (preferably Crown Royal) or bourbon

1 teaspoon vanilla extract or vanilla bean paste

1 teaspoon freshly grated nutmeg, plus more for garnish

In a large saucepan, heat 2½ cups of the cream over medium-low heat until it begins to steam but not boil. In a medium bowl, whisk the eggs with the sugar and salt. Using a heatproof measuring cup, measure out 1 cup of the hot cream. Gradually pour it into the egg mixture to temper, whisking constantly. In a slow, steady stream, pour the egg-cream mixture back into the saucepan with the hot cream. Continue to cook, whisking constantly over medium-low heat, until the mixture thickens enough to coat the back of a spoon, about 5 minutes. Strain through a fine-meshed sieve into a large bowl and let stand until cool, at least 15 minutes, stirring every few minutes. Stir in the rum, whiskey (or bourbon), vanilla, and the 1 teaspoon nutmeg. Finish preparing, or cover and refrigerate for up to 3 days.

To serve, use an electric mixer fitted with the whisk attachment to beat the remaining 1 cup cream until soft peaks form. Gently fold the whipped cream into the eggnog mixture. Transfer the eggnog to a pitcher and serve immediately. Top each serving with a sprinkling of fresh nutmeg.

TIP: The difference between freshly grated nutmeg and the finely ground stuff you find on the spice rack is enormous. Fresh nutmegs are available in the whole-spice section of most grocery stores. Grating the hard, round spice is much easier with gadgets made especially for grating nutmeg. Microplane and Zyliss make good ones.

Sweet Potato Scones

I love scones, and given the numerous plastic-wrapped dry, crumbly versions available at espresso stands everywhere, I think they are getting a bad reputation. The key to a good scone is cold butter, a light touch when mixing, and freshness. (In other words, for the most delicious results, eat your scones warm on the same day you make them.)

Although I've added the instructions for making the scones in a food processor, we always use our hands to make scones at the bakery. I think the hands-on approach makes for a more delicate scone, as long as you make sure not to overhandle the dough. As far as I am concerned, that's the point of baking—to get your hands in the dough.

{ Yield: 12 scones }

3 orange-fleshed sweet potatoes, about ¾ pound (see Tip)

4 cups all-purpose flour

⅔ cup sugar

1½ tablespoons baking powder

¼ teaspoon kosher salt

1 teaspoon ground cinnamon

½ teaspoon ground nutmeg

1 cup (2 sticks) cold unsalted butter, cut into tablespoon-sized slices

½ cup heavy whipping cream

½ cup buttermilk

Preheat the oven to 400°F. Lightly grease a baking sheet. Prick the sweet potatoes a few times with the tines of a fork and bake them on the prepared pan until tender, 30 to 40 minutes. Remove from the oven and let cool to the touch, about 10 minutes. Cut them in half lengthwise, scoop out the flesh into a medium bowl, and lightly mash with a fork. Cover the bowl and refrigerate until cool, at least 20 minutes. (Warm potatoes will melt the cold butter, keeping the scones from attaining optimum lightness and tenderness.)

Increase the oven temperature to 425°F. In a large bowl, combine the flour, sugar, baking powder, salt, cinnamon, and nutmeg. Use your hands or a pastry cutter to incorporate the butter into the flour mixture until the dough is crumbly and contains lumps the size of small peas. Add the cooled sweet potatoes and ¼ cup of the cream and lightly stir into the flour mixture. Add the remaining ¼ cup cream and the buttermilk and stir until just mixed. Do not overwork the dough.

Food processor method: In a food processor, mix the flour, sugar, baking powder, salt, cinnamon, and nutmeg. Add the butter and sweet potatoes to the flour mixture. Pulse until crumbly. With the machine running, gradually pour in the whipping cream and buttermilk. Stop the machine as soon as the liquid has been added. If the dough has begun to stick together in a ball, remove it. If not, add more cream, 1 tablespoon at a time, until the dough begins to form a ball.

continued

10

Place the dough on a lightly floured work surface. Lightly coat your hands with flour and form the dough into a ¾-inch-thick rectangle. Cut the dough into 6 squares, then cut each square on the diagonal to make triangle-shaped scones. Bake on an ungreased baking sheet for 15 to 20 minutes, until the scones are a light golden brown. Transfer to wire racks for cooling.

RATHER SWEET VARIATION

For a special holiday touch, give your scones a drizzle of maple cream. In a medium bowl, whisk together ¼ cup pure maple syrup, ¼ cup heavy whipping cream or half-and-half, 2 cups powdered sugar, and a pinch of kosher salt until smooth. Ice the warm scones by dipping the whisk in the maple cream and moving it quickly over the scones using a back-and-forth motion. Serve the scones warm or at room temperature.

TIP: I prefer sweet potatoes with orange flesh—they're sweeter and less starchy than the white- or yellow-fleshed varieties. Picking out the orange-fleshed type can be tricky as grocery stores often label them yams instead of sweet potatoes. Select the variety with the deepest orange skin available, regardless of the name.

Cranberry-Walnut Scones

Few people are blasé about walnuts. They either love 'em or hate 'em. I love them and almost always include them in these delicate scones. I do have a few customers who would rather eat worms than bite into a walnut, and if I know one of them is coming in, I leave out the walnuts. Frankly, these are fabulous either way. As always, scones are best served warm. If you can't serve them warm, at least serve them the same day you make them. Second-day scones are always second rate.

{ Yield: 12 scones }

½ cup walnuts

4 cups all-purpose flour

⅔ cup granulated sugar

2 tablespoons baking powder

1 teaspoon kosher salt

¾ cup (1½ sticks) cold unsalted butter, cut into tablespoon-sized pieces

2½ cups cold heavy whipping cream

2 cups fresh cranberries or sweetened dried cranberries

½ cup coarse natural sugar, such as Sugar in the Raw or turbinado, for sprinkling

Preheat the oven to 350°F. Arrange the walnuts on a rimmed baking sheet in a single layer and toast them in the oven for 7 to 9 minutes, until golden brown and aromatic. Transfer to a bowl and let cool. Coarsely chop the walnuts.

Increase the oven temperature to 425°F. In a large bowl, combine the flour, granulated sugar, baking powder, and salt. Use your hands or a pastry cutter to incorporate the butter into the flour mixture until it is crumbly and contains lumps the size of small peas. Add half of the cream and lightly stir it into the flour mixture. Add the remaining cream and stir until just mixed. Do not overwork the dough.

Food processor method: In a food processor, process the flour, granulated sugar, baking powder, and salt until combined. This should take about 30 seconds. Cut the butter into small bits (about ½-inch pieces) and add it to the flour mixture. Pulse 10 to 15 times, until crumbly with little bits of butter still intact. (Processing it too much will toughen the scones.) With the machine running, pour in the cream in a steady stream. Stop the machine as soon as the cream has been added. If the dough has begun to stick together in a ball, remove it. If a ball has not formed, pulse a few times until the dough begins to hold together. If it doesn't, add more cream, 1 tablespoon at a time, and pulse until the dough begins to form a ball.

Place the dough on a lightly floured work surface and gently knead in the cranberries and walnuts, handling the dough as little as possible. Form the dough into a ¾-inch-thick rectangle. Cut the dough into 6 even squares,

continued

13

then cut each square on the diagonal to make triangle-shaped scones. Top each scone with a sprinkling of coarse sugar. Place on an ungreased baking sheet and bake for about 20 minutes, until a light golden brown. Remove from the oven and transfer to wire racks. Serve warm or at room temperature.

Savory Rice Balls

I first tasted Mamie Fertitta's amazing rice balls at Mamie and Joe's food store, Jack's Pack-It. An old-fashioned neighborhood grocery store, it also featured a full butcher shop and a few of Mamie's prepared Italian specialties. Whenever I came home from college, one of the first things I'd do was stop by to see Mamie and her husband, Joe. Mamie knew I loved her rice balls, so as soon as she knew I was back in town, she'd make a fresh batch, wrap them individually, line them up neatly in clean shirt boxes, and give them to me. I could freeze them for later, or fry them up as soon as I got home. My parents had a charge account at Mamie and Joe's store, so as a kid I dropped by frequently to pick up things for the family. Many of the locals have charge accounts here at Rather Sweet, too, just like at Mamie's. Well, not exactly . . . when regular customers are short on cash they just tape the bill to the kitchen refrigerator and pay it later. After seven years in business, we've yet to be stiffed.

I know these are time-consuming, but they can be made ahead and deep-fried just before serving. For me, they are the ultimate comfort food. They are great on their own, but I frequently serve them with my all-purpose tomato sauce.

Panko crumbs are coarse, crisp Japanese bread crumbs, available in the ethnic food section of many grocery stores. When a recipe calls for bread crumbs, I almost always use panko crumbs because of their distinctive crisp texture. If you can't find them, use Italian-style or regular bread crumbs.

{ Yield: 15 to 20 medium balls }

7 cups water

1 teaspoon kosher salt

3 cups short- or medium-grain rice, such as pearl or glutinous

½ cup (1 stick) unsalted butter

¼ cup olive oil

1½ pounds lean ground beef

1 cup chopped yellow onion

1 cup finely chopped celery

2 cloves garlic, minced

2 tablespoons chili powder

One 15-ounce can tomato sauce

½ cup water

½ cup freshly grated Parmesan cheese

1 teaspoon kosher salt, or more to taste

½ teaspoon freshly ground pepper

2 tablespoons chopped fresh flat-leaf parsley

3 cups panko (Japanese bread crumbs) or Italian-style bread crumbs

1 tablespoon minced fresh oregano, or 2 teaspoons dried oregano

1 tablespoon minced fresh basil, or 2 teaspoons dried basil

6 large eggs

Canola oil for deep-frying

In a large saucepan, combine the water, salt, and rice and bring to a boil. Reduce the heat to low, cover, and simmer for about 25 minutes, or until the rice is slightly gummy. Remove from the heat, stir in the butter, and let cool uncovered.

In a large skillet, heat the ¼ cup olive oil over medium heat. Add the beef and sauté until browned. Add the onion, celery, and garlic. Reduce the heat to medium-low and cook for about 10 minutes. Stir in the chili powder, tomato sauce, and water. Simmer, uncovered, until thickened, about 1 hour. The mixture should be moist but not soupy. Stir in the Parmesan, salt, pepper, and half the parsley. Remove from the heat and let cool for at least 15 minutes.

Lightly coat your hands with butter. Place about 2 tablespoons rice in the cupped palm of one hand and mold the rice to resemble a small bowl. Spoon about 1 tablespoon of the meat mixture into the center. Mold the rice around the meat to cover it and shape it into a firm ball a little larger than a golf ball. Repeat to use all the remaining rice and meat. Place the balls on a baking sheet, cover with plastic wrap, and refrigerate for about an hour.

In a small bowl, stir together the bread crumbs, oregano, and basil. In another small bowl, beat the eggs with a fork until combined. Individually dip each rice ball in the egg mixture, then coat with the bread crumb mixture. Place on a baking sheet, cover, and refrigerate for at least 2 or up to 24 hours.

In a large, heavy saucepan or Dutch oven, heat about 3 inches of canola oil over medium-high heat to 350°F. Fry 2 or 3 rice balls at a time for 3 to 4 minutes per side, until crisp and golden brown. Transfer to paper towels to drain, then keep them warm in a low oven until all the balls are cooked. Serve warm, alone or set on a pool of tomato sauce.

Tomato Sauce

{ Yield: 4 cups }

2 tablespoons olive oil

1 cup chopped onion

3 cloves garlic, minced

4 cups (32-ounce can) puréed tomatoes

¼ cup water

1 teaspoon kosher salt

¼ cup minced fresh basil

1 tablespoon minced fresh oregano, or
    1 teaspoon dried oregano

2 teaspoons chili powder

Dash of Worcestershire sauce

Pinch of sugar

2 teaspoons cold unsalted butter

In a medium saucepan, heat the olive oil over medium heat. Add the onion and sauté until translucent, about 4 minutes. Stir in the garlic and sauté for 1 minute. Stir in the tomatoes, water, salt, basil, oregano, chili powder, Worcestershire, sugar, and butter. Cook until the mixture begins to boil, then reduce the heat to medium-low and simmer the sauce, uncovered, for 1 hour.

Mustard Baked Ham

Grandma made a mean ham that she served every Christmas. When I came upon this old family recipe, handwritten in my grandma's distinctive, compressed scrawl, I had to try it. I'm not a ham lover, but when I pulled this one from the oven I couldn't stop eating it. The lamb chops I'd planned for dinner went into the freezer.

You'll need an uncooked, bone-in country ham for this recipe. (Country hams by definition are salted and aged.) Few grocers stock country hams, but many will be happy to order one. I ordered from my neighborhood store and ended up with one of the oldest names in country ham, Smithfield. Soaking the ham overnight in water is critical, or the ham will taste too salty. Use the ham bone to make Split Pea Soup (page 21) when you're done with it.

{ Yield: About 10 servings }

One 5- to 6-pound uncooked, bone-in
    country ham
1 cup firmly packed brown sugar
½ cup Dijon mustard
1 cup fine fresh bread crumbs
½ cup panko crumbs (see headnote on
    page 16)
2 tablespoons cider vinegar
Whole cloves for decorating

Wash the ham and scrub it with a wire brush to remove any mold (harmless mold can be a by-product of curing). Put the ham in a large stockpot and add water to cover completely. Refrigerate for at least 12 or up to 24 hours.

Preheat the oven to 325°F. Remove the ham from the water, rinse it, and scrub it again with a stiff brush, if necessary. Pat the ham dry with paper towels. Place the ham, rind side up, on a wire rack in a roasting pan. Do not add water and do not cover. Bake the ham for about 20 minutes per pound, until an instant-read thermometer inserted in the ham but not touching bone registers 160° to 165°F. (It is imperative to cook the ham to this temperature to kill pathogens.)

Just before the ham is done, make the brown sugar paste: In a large bowl, combine the brown sugar, mustard, fresh bread crumbs, panko, and cider vinegar. Remove the ham from the oven and use a sharp knife to cut off the rind and any excess fat. Increase the oven temperature to 400°F. Place the ham back on the baking rack, fat side up. Evenly pat on the paste (no need to cover the bottom of the ham). Stick the cloves into the top surface of the ham. Bake for 15 to 20 minutes, until the paste turns golden brown and crispy. Remove the ham from the oven and let rest for 15 minutes.

Remove the cloves and carve the ham into thin slices. Serve with Fischer & Wieser's Honey Horseradish Mustard or their Sweet, Sour, and Smokey Mustard Sauce, available in many grocery stores, or go to their website at www.jelly.com.

Mamie's Marinated Green Bean and Artichoke Salad

I consider Mamie to be my Italian mama, even though we are not related by blood. Mamie and her husband, Joe, owned Jack's Pack-It, my family's favorite hometown food store. Mamie is a wonderful cook. When my ailing mother had a craving, sometimes only Mamie's cooking would do. (Her green bean and artichoke casserole was one of Mom's top choices.) Mamie kept the store open long after Joe died, and just recently sold it. The store was her whole life, and I think she misses it. I know all of her old friends from Beaumont, especially me, miss seeing her there.

This recipe is easy to make ahead and needs a few hours of marinating. It is even better if refrigerated overnight. Mamie's recipe calls for Italian dressing but doesn't include directions for making it, so I created a simple dressing. Hope you like it, Mamie.

{ Yield: 6 to 8 servings }

1 pound green beans, trimmed

One 14-ounce can artichoke hearts, well drained and quartered

3 stalks celery, thinly sliced

1 red bell pepper, seeded, deveined, and cut into large dice

½ cup kalamata olives, pitted and sliced

DRESSING

¼ cup good-quality Champagne vinegar

¾ cup extra-virgin olive oil

¾ teaspoon honey

¼ teaspoon Dijon mustard

Leaves from 1 oregano sprig, minced, or ¼ teaspoon dried oregano

1 clove garlic, minced

⅛ teaspoon kosher salt

⅛ teaspoon freshly ground pepper

Put the beans in a medium saucepan and add water to cover. Cover and bring to a boil over high heat. Cook for 4 to 5 minutes, or until crisp-tender. Drain the beans and plunge them into a bowl of cold water to stop them from cooking. Drain and dry them on paper towels. In a large bowl, stir together the artichoke hearts, beans, celery, red pepper, and olives.

To make the dressing: In a small bowl, whisk together the vinegar, olive oil, honey, mustard, oregano, garlic, salt, and pepper. Pour over the vegetables and toss to coat well. Cover and refrigerate for at least 3 hours or overnight.

♛ **TIP:** The dressing also can be made in a mini food processor, which eliminates the need to mince the garlic and oregano. Just whirl all the ingredients together until the garlic is minced and the dressing has emulsified.

Split Pea Soup

I hate to let a ham bone go to waste. It elevates standard split pea soup into a hearty, smoky delight, and it is very simple to make. The night after I serve a bone-in ham (see page 19), I carve any leftover ham from the bone and refrigerate the meat for sandwiches. Then the bone goes into a potful of water for a long simmer. Salt is not listed in the ingredients here for a good reason: The liquid absorbs plenty of salt from the ham bone as it simmers. Do not add salt to the soup until you've tasted it. It rarely needs supplementing.

{ Yield: 10 to 12 servings }

1 ham bone, carved clean

3 tablespoons unsalted butter

2 onions, chopped

2 stalks celery (leaves included), chopped

2 carrots, peeled and diced

1 pound split peas

Put the bone in a large stockpot and add water to cover. Bring to a boil, reduce the heat, cover, and simmer for at least 3 hours. (I often leave it to simmer overnight. I keep the heat at a low enough temperature to ensure the water won't boil off, leading to a ruined pot or worse.) Strain the ham stock into a large bowl.

Wash the stockpot and melt the butter in it over medium heat. Add the onions, celery, and carrots. Cook over medium heat until the onions are soft, about 10 minutes. Pour in the ham stock (there should be at least 10 cups). Add the split peas and simmer until soft, about 1 hour and 30 minutes. Purée about three-fourths of the soup using an immersion or regular blender. (Do not fill the regular blender more than half full, or the hot soup may spatter out the top and burn you.) Combine the purée with the remaining soup. Serve hot, in mugs or bowls.

Green Chile and Cheddar Baking Powder Biscuits

My grandmother always used to say, "Light hands make light biscuits," and she was right. I've learned through experience that overmixing leads to tough biscuits. That's why I mix biscuit dough with my hands: I can feel it when it's mixed just enough to hold together. Then I shape it and cut it into these wonderfully tender biscuits. Grandmother didn't serve these with her Christmas ham, but she should have. The green chiles give these biscuits a touch of holiday color and they complement her sweet-salty ham beautifully (see photo on page 18).

{ Yield: About 12 biscuits }

4 cups all-purpose flour

2 tablespoons baking powder

1 heaping teaspoon kosher salt

1 tablespoon sugar

1 cup shredded sharp Cheddar cheese

4 tablespoons cold unsalted butter, plus melted butter for brushing

5 tablespoons vegetable shortening

1⅓ cups milk

One 7-ounce can chopped green chiles, drained

Preheat the oven to 450°F. Grease a baking sheet with butter or cooking spray.

In a large bowl, mix the flour, baking powder, salt, sugar, and cheese until combined. Add the butter and vegetable shortening and work with your hands or a pastry cutter until crumbly with visible bits of butter or shortening about the size of baby peas. Make a well in the center of the flour mixture and add the milk and green chiles. Stir the dough just until it can be formed into a soft ball.

On a floured work surface, lightly press the dough into a disk about 1¼ inches thick. Dip a 3-inch biscuit cutter in flour and cut out biscuits as close together as possible. Mold the scraps into a small disk and cut out the rest of the biscuits. Place the biscuits on the prepared pan. Using a pastry brush, spread a light layer of melted butter on the biscuit tops.

Bake for 12 to 15 minutes, until the biscuits are golden brown.

♔ **TIP:** My grandmother used a combination of vegetable shortening and butter, which combine to create the tenderest of biscuits. For the past few years, I've tried to avoid most commercial vegetable shortening, which is made with partially hydrogenated oil, recently shown to be worse for our hearts than regular saturated fat. Instead, I use organic nonhydrogenated vegetable shortening, available in most natural foods stores and in many upscale grocery stores. My brand (Spectrum) is made from palm oil and contains no trans fats.

Creamy Chicken Lasagna

When out-of-town relatives descend for the holidays, I make at least one batch of lasagna. It's sure to please the most finicky eater, and this recipe makes enough to feed the hungriest horde. My lasagna is an utterly decadent one, filled with butter, cream, and plenty of cheese. My customers love it—leaving me no choice but to make it at least once a week. If you like to shave fat from recipes, this one can take it with ease. I make several versions for catering jobs, and two are listed at the end of this recipe. Like most homemade lasagnas, this one is time-consuming. It can be made in advance and kept in the refrigerator, unbaked, for 1 day. Make sure to increase the baking time by about 10 minutes if the lasagna goes directly from the refrigerator to the oven.

{ Yield: 8 to 10 servings }

CREAM SAUCE

2 tablespoons olive oil

1 yellow onion, chopped

2 stalks celery, diced

10 ounces button mushrooms, sliced

1 red bell pepper, seeded, deveined, and diced

3 cloves garlic, minced

2 tablespoons chopped fresh flat-leaf parsley

2 teaspoons kosher salt

½ teaspoon freshly ground pepper to taste

1 cup (2 sticks) unsalted butter

2 cups all-purpose flour

3 cups chicken stock

1 cup heavy whipping cream

1 cup freshly grated Parmesan cheese

2 shakes Tabasco sauce

2 teaspoons kosher salt

1 teaspoon ground white pepper

Pinch of ground nutmeg

15 lasagna noodles (about 12 ounces)

1 rotisserie chicken, skinned, deboned, and shredded into bite-sized pieces

3 cups (12 ounces) shredded Monterey jack cheese

1 cup freshly grated Parmesan cheese

Preheat the oven to 350°F. Grease a 9 by 13-inch baking dish with butter or cooking spray.

To make the cream sauce: In a large sauté pan, heat the olive oil over medium heat. Add the onion, celery, mushrooms, red pepper, and garlic and sauté until the onion is translucent, about 5 minutes. Stir in the parsley, salt, and pepper. Remove from the heat and set aside.

In a large sauté pan or stockpot, melt the butter over medium-low heat. Whisk in the flour ½ cup at a time, whisking after each addition until smooth. Add the chicken stock 1 cup at a time, whisking after each addition until smooth. Increase the heat to medium and cook the sauce until it thickens to the consistency

of a cream soup. Stir in the cream, Parmesan, Tabasco, salt, pepper, and nutmeg and heat until the cheese is completely melted. Stir in the sautéed vegetables and remove from the heat.

In a large pot of salted boiling water, cook the lasagna noodles according to the package directions. Drain the noodles and separate them. (I hang them around the edges of the cooking pot.)

Spread a thin layer of cream sauce over the bottom of the prepared baking dish. Layer 5 lasagna noodles on top, then layer with half of the chicken, 1 cup of the jack cheese, and one-third of the remaining cream sauce. Layer 5 more noodles on top and continue with the rest of the chicken, 1 cup jack cheese, and one-third of the cream sauce. Layer on the last 5 noodles and cover them with the remaining cream sauce. Mix together the Parmesan and the remaining cup of jack cheese. Sprinkle the cheese evenly over the top of the lasagna.

Bake for 30 to 45 minutes, until the lasagna is bubbling. Remove from the oven and let stand for 15 minutes before cutting and serving.

RATHER SWEET VARIATIONS

For a lower-fat version, cut the butter and flour in half (1 stick butter, 1 cup flour) and substitute low-fat or nonfat milk for the whipping cream. Leave out the Monterey jack cheese altogether and use only the Parmesan.

For a festive spinach and prosciutto version, place 10 ounces washed and drained spinach in a medium saucepan. (The water left on the leaves is enough to steam it.) Cook on medium to medium-low heat for 3 to 4 minutes, until the spinach is wilted. Follow the directions above for the lasagna. Cover the final layer of chicken and cheese with an even layer of spinach, then an even layer of thinly sliced prosciutto. Add the final lasagna noodles and cheese. Bake as directed above.

Pear and Apricot Jam Bars

Not just for the holidays, these rich bars easily can change with the seasons, showcasing whatever fruit variety is best at the time. Peaches, apples, or fresh berries will work in place of pears. Use whatever jam or marmalade you think will complement the main fruit selection. Almond paste is a mixture of ground blanched almonds and sweeteners and can be found in most grocery stores. It's not everyone's favorite; leave it out if a vocal critic lives in your home.

{ Yield: About 2 dozen bars }

CRUST

1 cup (2 sticks) cold unsalted butter, cut into tablespoon-sized pieces

¾ cup firmly packed brown sugar

2½ cups all-purpose flour

¼ teaspoon kosher salt

½ cup sliced almonds

FILLING

1 cup apricot jam

5 to 6 firm pears (I use Bartlett), peeled, cored, and cut into ¼-inch-thick slices

1 cup fresh or frozen cranberries (optional)

TOPPING

½ cup firmly packed brown sugar

2 cups all-purpose flour

¼ teaspoon kosher salt

1 cup (2 sticks) cold unsalted butter, cut into tablespoon-sized pieces

1 cup (8 ounces) almond paste

1 cup sliced almonds

To make the crust: Preheat the oven to 350°F. Coat the inside of a 9 by 13-inch baking pan with butter or cooking spray. In a food processor, pulse the butter, sugar, flour, salt, and almonds just until the mixture is crumbly, with butter bits the size of peas. Press the crust evenly over the bottom of the prepared pan and bake for 20 to 25 minutes, until the crust is golden brown.

To make the filling: Spread the apricot jam evenly over the top of the crust. Arrange the pears (overlapping if you want more fruit, or side by side for less) evenly over the top of the jam. Sprinkle evenly with the cranberries, if you like.

To make the topping: In a food processor, combine the sugar, flour, and salt and process to blend. Add the butter and pulse until crumbly. Break the almond paste into pieces and add with the almond slices to the food processor. Pulse a few times, making sure to leave some larger pieces (at least pea-sized) of almond paste intact. Spread this mixture evenly over the sliced pears. Bake for 20 to 25 minutes, until the bars are bubbling and the crumb topping is golden brown. Remove from the oven and let cool for at least 2 hours before cutting into squares. Wrapped bars will keep for up to 1 week in the refrigerator.

RATHER SWEET VARIATION

Don't be afraid to experiment with this recipe. I make it in many ways, with many different fruits, nuts, and jams. I love peaches matched with pecans; apples are great with walnuts and a touch of cinnamon; and I often match pears with currant jam for a touch of Christmas red. I'm not a fan of mixing different kinds of nuts in this recipe, so I always omit the almond paste when using anything other than almonds.

Aunt Milbry's Fruitcake

This is not your typical holiday fruitcake. Why? Because I can't stand the traditional versions, filled with lurid, artificially colored candied fruit, or mincemeat (horrors!). Then there is the cake's texture, often as tough and dry as a West Texas cowboy. Still, I felt honor-bound to include a fruitcake recipe in this book. After all, holiday fruitcake is a venerable Southern tradition. Luckily, I stumbled on a recipe from my Great-Aunt Milbry—an expert cook, according to all who knew her. Aunt Milbry's recipe looked promising—butter was the first listed ingredient, and diced Granny Smith apples were included. I made a few changes, substituting dried Calimyrna figs for the mincemeat and dried cranberries for the candied fruit. The result is a moist, dense, and darkly wonderful fruitcake (see photo on page 168).

Unlike most baked goods, fruitcake improves with age. This version must be made in advance and should not be cut or eaten until completely cool. I like to wrap the cooled cake in heavy-duty foil and keep it in the refrigerator for a few weeks. Every week, I open the top and brush on a little brandy to keep it moist.

{ Yield: 12 to 14 servings }

¾ cup (1½ sticks) unsalted butter at room temperature

1 cup sugar

3 large eggs

1 teaspoon vanilla extract

2 cups all-purpose flour

1 tablespoon baking soda

½ teaspoon kosher salt

1 unpeeled Granny Smith apple, cored and diced

2 cups pecans, toasted and chopped

1 cup chopped dates

1 cup chopped Calimyrna figs

1 cup mixed dried fruit, such as cranberries, cherries, blueberries, golden raisins, chopped apricots, or chopped peaches

¾ cup thick high-quality preserves, such as apricot, pear, peach, or fig

Brandy for brushing on top of the baked cake (optional)

Preheat the oven to 275°F. Grease a 10-inch angel food cake pan with butter or cooking spray.

Using an electric mixer fitted with the paddle attachment, cream the butter and the sugar on medium-high speed until light and fluffy, about 2 minutes. Add the eggs and vanilla and beat for 1 minute. Add the flour, baking soda, and salt and beat on low speed until just combined. Stir in the apple, pecans, dried fruits, and preserves.

Bake for 1½ hours, or until the cake pulls away from the sides of the pan. (It may have a few wet areas where the jam is concentrated, but it will firm up as it cools.) Remove from the oven and let cool completely in the pan; this will take a few hours. Using a pastry brush, paint a light layer of brandy on top of the cooled

cake, if you like. Wrap the cake in heavy-duty aluminum foil and refrigerate for up to 2 months, brushing with the optional brandy once a week.

TIP: For an elegant dessert, slice the fruitcake and serve with bourbon whipped cream: Using an electric mixer fitted with the whisk attachment, beat 2 cups heavy whipping cream until stiff peaks form. Stir in 2 tablespoons bourbon and 2 tablespoons powdered sugar. Serve immediately atop a slice of fruitcake.

RATHER SWEET VARIATION

Once your friends have tasted this fruitcake, they'll be thrilled to receive one as a gift. Follow the recipe as above, but bake the batter in small loaf pans for about 1 hour and 15 minutes. Let the cakes cool, then wrap them in plastic wrap or cellophane. Set a fruitcake in the middle of a large square of holiday tissue paper, and tie with a bow that has been wrapped around a mini bottle of your favorite brandy. For another idea for wrapping individual fruitcakes, see page 169. Makes 6 mini loaves (6 by 3 by 2 inches).

Red Velvet Cupcakes with Mascarpone Cream Cheese Icing

Although legend has it that the red velvet cake originated in the early 1900s at New York City's Waldorf Astoria Hotel, it's been a Southern favorite for as long as I can remember. (A friend of mine recently reported seeing a version of it at a Starbucks in Mississippi.) Years ago, I made an armadillo-shaped red velvet cake for a wedding couple, complete with gray cream cheese icing for the animal's shell and scales. The idea may have come from the popular 1989 movie Steel Magnolias, which featured a red velvet armadillo groom's cake, a popular Southern tradition that continues to this day.

The inspiration for my red velvet cupcakes came from my high-school boyfriend's grandmother. My mother was quite ill during those years, so I spent a lot of time with Bob Yarborough's family. His Birmingham, Alabama–born grandmother cooked and baked frequently, and I never forgot her red velvet cake. I wrote the instructions in my high-school recipe notebook and used it as a guide for developing these cupcakes.

The mint extract and crushed mint candies add bit of holiday flair, but easily can be left out at other times of the year.

{ Yield: 12 Texas-sized cupcakes }

¼ cup (2 ounces) red food coloring

3½ tablespoons high-quality unsweetened cocoa powder

1 cup (2 sticks) unsalted butter at room temperature

1¾ cups sugar

2 large eggs

2 cups cake flour

1½ cups all-purpose flour

1 teaspoon kosher salt

1 teaspoon baking soda

2 teaspoons vanilla extract

1 cup buttermilk

1 cup sour cream

1 tablespoon distilled white vinegar

ICING

1 cup (2 sticks) unsalted butter at room temperature

1 cup (8 ounces) cream cheese at room temperature

2 cups powdered sugar

1 teaspoon vanilla extract

Pinch of kosher salt

1 cup (8 ounces) mascarpone (Italian cream cheese, available at most grocery stores)

1 teaspoon vanilla or mint extract

Crushed peppermint candy for garnish (optional)

continued

Preheat the oven to 350°F. Grease jumbo muffin cups (3½ inches in diameter and 2 inches deep) with butter or cooking spray, and lightly flour them, knocking out the excess flour, or line them with baking papers.

In a small bowl, stir the food coloring and cocoa powder together to make a smooth paste. Set aside. Using an electric mixer fitted with the paddle attachment, cream the butter and the sugar on medium-high speed until light and fluffy, about 2 minutes. Add the eggs, one at a time, beating after each addition, then add the cocoa paste while continuing to beat. Reduce the mixer speed to medium and beat the batter for about 4 minutes. In a medium bowl, sift together the cake flour, all-purpose flour, salt, and baking soda. Stir the vanilla into the buttermilk (this can be done in the measuring cup). Add the flour mixture in 3 increments alternately with the buttermilk in 2 increments, starting and ending with the flour. Beat on medium speed just until the ingredients are combined. Add the sour cream and vinegar and beat on low speed until combined.

Fill the muffin cups three-fourths full with batter. Bake for 25 to 35 minutes, just until the cupcakes feel firm to the touch and a toothpick inserted in the center comes out clean. Do not overbake, or the cupcakes will dry out. Remove from the oven and let cool in the pans for 5 minutes, then unmold onto a wire rack and let cool completely before frosting.

To make the icing: In the large bowl of an electric mixer fitted with the paddle attachment, beat the butter, cream cheese, and powdered sugar on medium-high speed until light and fluffy. Beat in the mascarpone on very low speed until just combined. (Be careful; once you've added the mascarpone, excessive beating can make the frosting curdle.) Stir in the vanilla or mint extract.

Frost the top of each muffin with the icing. Sprinkle the crushed peppermint candy, if using, evenly on the cupcakes.

King-Sized Key Lime Pie

Customers have been begging me for this recipe ever since we opened. It's a standard Key lime pie recipe, but I make it with an ultrathick graham cracker crust studded with chopped macadamia nuts. For a dramatic, holiday-worthy dessert, place the pie on a large plate or cake stand, and surround it with a double row of fresh cranberries.

You'll need a 10-inch tart pan with a removable bottom and fluted edges that stands at least 2 inches high. If you can't find one in your local baking supply store, Williams-Sonoma carries them.

Fresh Key limes are difficult to get outside of the South. You can buy bottled Key lime juice in many upscale grocery stores, but I prefer the fresh . When I can't find fresh Key limes, which is often, I substitute the more commonly available Persian limes. The pie still tastes great.

{ Yield: 8 large servings }

CRUST

1 cup macadamia nuts

3¾ cups graham cracker crumbs (about 30 crackers)

1 teaspoon sugar

1 cup (2 sticks) salted butter, melted

FILLING

3 large egg yolks

1½ cups freshly squeezed lime juice (about 6 limes)

3½ cups sweetened condensed milk

1 tablespoon high-quality light rum (optional)

WHIPPED CREAM TOPPING

2 cups cold heavy whipping cream

½ cup powdered sugar

1 large lime, scrubbed

To make the crust: Preheat the oven to 300°F. Coat a 10 by 2-inch tart pan with a removable bottom with cooking spray. Arrange the macadamia nuts on a rimmed baking sheet in a single layer and toast them in the oven for 7 to 9 minutes, until golden brown and aromatic. Remove from the oven, transfer to a bowl, let cool, and coarsely chop.

In a large bowl, stir together the graham cracker crumbs, sugar, butter, and macadamia nuts. Press the dough evenly into the bottom and all the way up the sides of the prepared pan. The crust should be between ¼ and ½ inch thick throughout.

To make the filling: In a large bowl, whisk together the egg yolks, lime juice, condensed milk, and rum until thoroughly combined. Pour into the prepared crust and bake for 30 to 35 minutes, until the crust is a light golden brown and the filling is partially set. Remove

continued

from the oven and let cool, then refrigerate the pie overnight so that it sets up thoroughly.

To make the whipped cream topping: Using an electric mixer fitted with the whisk attachment, beat the cream in a large bowl on high speed until soft peaks form. Add the powdered sugar and whip until stiff peaks form and the sugar is thoroughly blended in. Spoon half the whipped cream into a pastry bag fitted with a large star tip. Hold the pastry bag near the edge of the pie and make tight circles with the bag to create 8 evenly spaced rosettes of whipped cream around the edge of the pie; each rosette should be about 2 inches high and 2½ inches wide.

Cut the lime into 8 thin crosswise slices, then cut each slice from the rind's edge to the center of the slice. (You do not want to cut the circle in half.) Pick up the slice and twist each side of the cut in the opposite direction. Place a twisted lime slice on top of each whipped cream rosette. Refrigerate until ready to serve.

TIP: I have yet to find commercially available graham cracker crumbs made without partially hydrogenated oils—a no-no in my food ingredients book. I buy graham crackers at my nearby natural foods store, after checking the label carefully to ensure they don't contain the offending fats, then use my food processor to transform them into crumbs: Break the crackers in half, add them to the processor about 10 at a time, and whirl them around until they become fine crumbs. Add the macadamias and pulse them in the food processor until coarsely chopped.

36

Tiny Whiskey-Glazed Eggnog Cakes

These whiskey-spiked bite-sized cakes are both festive and hard to resist—a perfect addition to a holiday buffet. I adapted an old family recipe for pound cake to make them. If you wish, make them ahead of time and freeze them before glazing. Well wrapped, they'll keep in the freezer for about 3 weeks. Defrost them, prick a few holes in the top of each cake with a toothpick, glaze, and serve.

{ Yield: About 3 dozen cakes }

1 cup (2 sticks) unsalted butter at room temperature

3 cups sugar

6 large eggs

1 teaspoon vanilla extract

1 teaspoon kosher salt

3 cups all-purpose flour

1 cup heavy whipping cream

¼ cup whiskey (I use Crown Royal)

2 teaspoons freshly grated nutmeg

WHISKEY GLAZE

¼ cup milk

¼ cup whiskey

3 cups powdered sugar

Freshly grated nutmeg for garnish

Preheat the oven to 325°F. Grease standard (2-inch-diameter) muffin pans with butter. Dust the pans with flour and knock out the excess. Alternately, use Baker's Joy or line the pans with baking papers. Using an electric mixer fitted with the paddle attachment, beat the butter and sugar in a large bowl on medium speed until light and fluffy, about 2 minutes. Scrape down the sides of the bowl and add the eggs, one at a time, beating until incorporated after each addition. Beat in the vanilla and salt. Turn the speed to low and add the flour 1 cup at a time, beating until incorporated after each addition.

In a medium bowl, using an electric mixer fitted with the whisk attachment, beat the cream until soft peaks form. Using a large rubber spatula, fold the whipped cream into the butter mixture. Fold in the whiskey and nutmeg.

Fill the muffin pans three-fourths full with batter. Do not overfill the pans, or the muffins will be difficult to remove. Top each with a sprinkling of nutmeg. Bake for 25 to 30 minutes, until golden brown around the edges. Remove from the oven and let cool in the pans for 5 minutes, then unmold on wire racks to cool completely.

To make the whiskey glaze: Whisk together the milk, whiskey, and powdered sugar until combined. Drizzle over the cakes.

Garnish with a sprinkling of nutmeg. The cakes can be served immediately, or left until the glaze dries.

Panna Cotta Parfaits with Hibiscus-Berry Compote

I first learned about panna cotta, the wonderful dessert from Italy's Piedmont region, when I worked as the executive pastry chef for restaurateur Tony Vallone in Houston. I loved it for several reasons. For one thing, it's so versatile you can change it up in infinite ways—with a touch of chocolate or caramel sauce, a sprinkling of fresh berries or vanilla bean paste. You can add rum, brandy, or any liqueur. Heavy cream is its main ingredient, but sour cream, crème fraîche, buttermilk, mascarpone, or even yogurt can be added in small amounts to make the dessert richer or tangier.

{ Yield: 6 servings }

1 envelope unflavored gelatin

½ cup milk

2 cups heavy whipping cream

2 vanilla beans, split lengthwise

¾ cup powdered sugar

½ cup sour cream

2 tablespoons Cognac (optional)

COMPOTE

6 hibiscus teabags, or 4 heaping
   tablespoons dried hibiscus

2 cups boiling water

1 cup granulated sugar

2 cups mixed dried cranberries, cherries,
   and blueberries

Sprinkle the gelatin over the milk in a measuring cup. Let the mixture soften (without stirring) for 5 minutes. In a medium saucepan, combine cream and vanilla beans and heat over medium-low heat just until barely steaming, not boiling or simmering. Whisk in the powdered sugar and heat until warm. Whisk in the gelatin mixture, then the sour cream.

Remove from the heat and stir in the Cognac. Pour the panna cotta into individual glasses (see Tip). Let cool, then refrigerate until set, at least 2 hours.

To make the compote: Put the teabags or dried hibiscus in a medium saucepan and pour the boiling water over. Let steep for 5 minutes. Remove the teabags or strain out the hibiscus. Stir in the sugar. Bring to a simmer over medium heat and cook for 7 to 8 minutes, until the syrup thickens slightly. Remove from the heat and stir in the dried fruit. Refrigerate until completely cool, about 2 hours.

Spoon compote in the center of each chilled panna cotta and serve. (You can cover the entire top of the panna cotta or let a bit of panna cotta show around the edges of the fruit.) You will have extra sauce, a minor blessing, as it is fabulous on ice cream or frozen yogurt, pound cake, or pancakes. It will keep in the refrigerator for about 1 month.

continued

TIP: I love to serve this panna cotta in stemmed glassware, but this wonderful dessert tastes and looks great no matter how you serve it. Try individual ramekins, short cocktail glasses, or even espresso cups complete with matching saucers and tiny espresso spoons. (Most espresso cups are not large enough to hold ½-cup servings, so adjust the servings accordingly.)

Mr. Vallone's Italian Cookies

In 1989, Houston restaurateur Tony Vallone hired me to become his executive pastry chef and gave me my first personalized chef's jacket. I've never forgotten it, or the four years I spent working for him. Always professional, always in command, and supremely successful, Mr. Vallone at one time owned four of Houston's top restaurants. (He has since sold three of them.) I learned much under his tutelage and am grateful to him for it. Recently Mr. Vallone (I would never call him anything else) opened Tony's, a glamorous restaurant in Houston's Greenway Plaza. He hired me as a consultant to develop new desserts for his menu. When I entered the restaurant I was amazed that many of the people I had worked with more than ten years earlier were still there. I spent a few days working with Mr. Vallone's talented chef Olivier Ciesielski. Before I left, Mr. Vallone treated me to a sumptuous multicourse lunch. "I'm glad you are back," he said. "You haven't lost your touch." Neither has he. And his words of praise mean more to me than he may know.

These cookies, known in Italy as pignoli cookies, are popular with both Italians and Americans. They are simple, easy to make, and freeze beautifully. For those who worry about such things, they also happen to be gluten-free. I find it hard to stop eating them.

{ Yield: About 4 dozen cookies }

2 cans (8 ounces each) almond paste
2 cups powdered sugar
½ teaspoon kosher salt
2 large egg whites
2 tablespoons honey
1 cup pine nuts (pignoli)

Preheat the oven to 350°F. Line baking sheets with silicone mats or parchment paper that has been well greased with cooking spray. (Do not bake these cookies on plain greased baking sheets, or they will be impossible to remove in one piece.) Using an electric mixer fitted with the paddle attachment, mix the almond paste, sugar, and salt on medium speed until crumbly, about 1 minute. Add the egg whites and honey and beat on medium speed for 5 minutes.

Using a 1-inch scoop, drop mounds of dough ½ inch apart on the prepared pans. Press pine nuts into the cookies to evenly cover the tops and sides. (This is painstaking work, because no one I know has yet to devise a way to press in more than just a few pine nuts at a time. Persevere, knowing that you'll be rewarded when these beautiful, rounded cookies emerge from the oven studded with lightly golden nuts.) Bake for 12 to 15 minutes, until the cookies are a deep golden brown around the edges. Remove from the oven and let cool completely before removing the cookies from the pans with a metal spatula. Store in an air-tight container for up to 3 days, or wrap and freeze for up to 1 month.

TIP: Pine nuts are expensive, and because they are relatively high in fat, they go rancid easily. I save money by buying them in large bags at Costco and freezing whatever I don't use immediately. They can be frozen for up to 9 months.

Outdoor Tree Trimming

Use things you already have around the house and buy a lot of greenery is my motto when it comes to decorating for the holidays. I fill my prettiest bowls with ornaments or fruit, turn old silver trophies into candy cane holders, and transform food into Christmas ornaments. My business partner, Dan Kamp, and I buy plenty of cedar boughs, and we use them to dress up windows, ledges, and flower boxes. Christmas paraphernalia that we've collected over the years nestles in the boughs and looks gorgeous against the green background.

I think decorating demands a celebration, and most years we throw a small tree-trimming party for our staff. We provide the food—In-the-Bag Chili Frito Pie (page 44) and Rather Minty Brownies (page 46)—and our wait staff helps us dress up the bakery for Christmas. We string outdoor Christmas lights, and last year we erected a twelve-foot tree in the bakery courtyard. Since food is our business, we naturally gravitate toward edible ornaments. We use fresh fruit, dried fruit, chiles, and tortillas, as well as garlands strung with gummy bears, gum drops, and fresh cranberries.

TO MAKE FRESH FRUIT ORNAMENTS:
Use red or green ribbon to tie a knot around the stems of apples, poblano chiles, pears, or any stemmed fruit of your choice. Tie another knot to secure the fruit to branches on a Christmas tree.

TO MAKE DRIED FRUIT ORNAMENTS:
Set the oven at its lowest temperature. Grease a baking sheet with cooking spray or line it with a silicone mat. Slice apples, pears, grapefruit, lemons, limes, or oranges as thinly as possible. (Use a mandoline, if you have one. Otherwise, do the best you can with a sharp knife.) Dip the sliced fruit in lemon-lime soda to keep it from discoloring. Punch a small hole near the top edge of each slice with a skewer. Lay the fruit slices in a single layer on the prepared pan and bake for 4 hours, or until the slices are completely dried. Slip a metal ornament hook through the hole in each fruit slice and hang it on the tree.

TO MAKE TORTILLA ORNAMENTS:
Buy a package of corn or flour tortillas and cut them into shapes with cookie cutters. Punch a hole near the top of the tortilla ornament with a skewer. Fill a heavy sauté pan with ½ inch of canola oil and set it over medium-high heat

until a tortilla scrap added to the oil sizzles and quickly turns a light golden brown. Use tongs to add the remaining tortilla shapes in batches, frying for 8 to 10 seconds on each side, until a light golden brown. Using a slotted metal spatula, transfer the shapes to paper towels to drain. Slip a metal ornament hook through the hole in each tortilla and hang it on the tree.

TO MAKE CRANBERRY, GUMMY BEAR, AND GUMDROP GARLANDS: Thread heavy-gauge cotton thread on an appropriately sized needle and alternately string fresh cranberries, gummy bears, and gumdrops.

In-the-Bag Chili Frito Pie

My customers love chili, and I often make it a couple of times a week. Still, they clamor for more. After a little experimentation, I have perfected a chili that is worth cooking daily. Apart from the dried chiles, there are two secret ingredients: bittersweet chocolate and a touch of masa harina, the dried-corn flour used to make tortillas and tamales.

I have provided a range for the chili powder to allow for differing levels of heat tolerance. Start conservatively and add powder to taste. And when working with dried chiles, take care to remove all the seeds, unless you crave the added fire.

Yield: 8 servings

2 ancho chiles (1 tablespoon ancho chile powder is a fine substitute)

2 dried Anaheim chiles

1 dried chipotle chile

4 slices bacon (I use applewood smoked)

1 large yellow onion, diced

5 cloves garlic, minced

1 pound ground sirloin

1 pound coarsely ground or regular ground beef

2 to 4 tablespoons chili powder

2 teaspoons dried Mexican oregano

1½ to 2 teaspoons kosher salt

½ teaspoon cayenne pepper

1 teaspoon red pepper flakes

2 shakes Tabasco sauce

3 ounces bittersweet chocolate, chopped

One 28-ounce can pureed tomatoes

1 to 1½ cups beef stock

2 tablespoons masa harina mixed with 1 tablespoon water (or more as needed to make a smooth paste)

1 cup (4 ounces) shredded sharp Cheddar cheese for serving

1 large red onion, diced, for serving

2 cups sour cream for serving

8 individual lunch-sized bags Fritos or other corn chips

Preheat the oven to 350°F and line a baking sheet with aluminum foil. Toast the ancho, Anaheim, and chipotle chiles on the prepared pan until crisp, about 10 minutes. Pull off and discard the stems, shake out the seeds, and grind the peppers in a food processor or spice grinder.

In a large sauté pan, fry the bacon over medium heat for about 3 minutes. Add the onion and

garlic and cook until the onion is translucent, about 10 minutes. Remove the bacon and use it to make a BLT for lunch. Increase the heat to medium-high and brown the beef with the onion and garlic in the bacon drippings. Using a large spoon, remove as much of the leftover fat as possible. Stir in the ground chiles, chili powder, oregano, salt, cayenne pepper, red pepper flakes, Tabasco, and chocolate. Cook over medium heat for 2 minutes. Stir in the tomatoes and beef stock. Simmer, uncovered, over low heat for about 1½ hours. Stir in the masa harina mixture and cook for another 10 minutes.

Serve with bowls of Cheddar cheese, red onion, and sour cream. Open each Fritos bag from the top, then split the seam and turn both flaps back diagonally so the Fritos are exposed. Spoon a generous helping of chili on top and let guests add the toppings of their choice.

♕ **TIP:** Texans are persnickety about chili. They like it hot, and they do not like it with beans. There's an unwritten law in Texas that chili must not contain beans. People from other parts of the country may feel differently, and I respect that. If you really love beans, I suggest you serve this with a steaming pot of bacon-flavored pinto beans. That may not satisfy all of you, so go ahead and add a can or two of drained kidney beans to the chili itself if you must. But as a Texan, I have to draw the line somewhere: Please don't call it chili.

Rather Minty Brownies

I wanted to make a minty holiday brownie that would appeal to kids. After a few tries that didn't hit the mark, I added Junior Mints, a perennial kid favorite. But an informal poll conducted at the bakery uncovered several kids who turn their noses up at mint in any form. I had to come up with a variation. It turns out that brownies lend themselves to all kinds of kid-friendly candies. You are welcome to experiment for yourself. I've already discovered that mini peanut butter cups work well (see Variation). Whatever you add, cut these utterly rich and fudgy brownies small. Overdoses are possible.

Although these brownies come together quickly, it's important to make them in advance. They are so fudgy that they are almost impossible to cut or serve until they've cooled and spent at least 1 hour in the freezer.

Yield: About 2 dozen brownies

1 cup (2 sticks) unsalted butter

6 ounces bittersweet chocolate (at least 60 percent cocoa content), chopped

2 cups sugar

4 large eggs

1½ cups all-purpose flour

1 teaspoon kosher salt

2 teaspoons vanilla extract

4 packages (1.84 ounces each) Junior Mints or other chocolate-covered mint candies

Preheat the oven to 350°F. Line a 9 by 13-inch pan with aluminum foil and grease it with butter or cooking spray.

In a large saucepan, melt the butter and chocolate over medium-low heat just until melted. (Make sure not to let the chocolate boil or burn, or it will give the brownies a bitter flavor.) Remove from the heat and let cool for about 10 minutes. Add the sugar, eggs, flour, salt, and vanilla all at once. Stir until completely combined. Pour into the prepared pan. Arrange the Junior Mints in even rows over the top. (I do 8 across and 10 down.)

Bake for about 25 minutes, until the brownies pull away from the sides of the pan. Let cool completely in the pan. Freeze, uncovered, for at least 1 hour, or until firm enough to cut easily. Lift the brownies out of the pan using the edges of the foil as handles. (If the brownies are not firm enough to keep from breaking as you lift them out, return them to the freezer until they are solid.) Cut into small squares and place on a serving plate in 1 layer. (They are so soft that they will stick together if stacked.)

👑 **TIP:** My coauthor, Alison, has a friend who asks for frozen Junior Mints at every movie theater she visits (most theaters seem to offer them). Soon, she became a frozen Junior Mint addict herself and suggested I try freezing these brownies. I wrapped the brownies individually in aluminum foil, froze them, and ate them straight from the freezer. I highly recommend it.

RATHER SWEET VARIATION

For peanut butter cup brownies, substitute about 35 mini peanut butter cups for the Junior Mints. Place the peanut butter cups in rows 5 across and 7 down. Push them into the batter so that just the tops are showing. Bake as directed above.

Coconut Snowballs

Busy holiday bakers need at least one recipe for a delicious no-bake cookie to liberate them from oven duty. This dainty is perfect for a tea or cookie swap, and it stirs together on top of the stove in a jiffy. The puffed rice cereal gives the cookies a distinctive crunch, and you can use the leftover egg whites to make My Mistake Cookies (see facing page).

Yield: About 4 dozen cookies

½ cup (1 stick) unsalted butter

2 large egg yolks

⅔ cup sugar

1 pound chopped dates

1 teaspoon vanilla extract

¼ teaspoon kosher salt

2 cups puffed rice cereal

1 cup chopped pecans

Sweetened shredded coconut for coating

In a large saucepan, combine the butter, egg yolks, and sugar. Stir over medium-low heat until the butter melts. Add the dates and continue cooking and stirring for about 5 minutes. (The dough will be difficult to stir, but persevere as best you can.) Remove from the heat and stir in the vanilla, salt, puffed rice, and pecans. Roll the dough into bite-sized balls (about 1 inch in diameter). Roll the balls in the shredded coconut to coat. The cookies will keep for up to 1 week in an airtight container or up to 1 month well wrapped and frozen.

My Mistake Cookies

Developing recipes can be a tricky business. I got a fresh reminder of this after tasting a cookie that I wanted to re-create. I had a pretty good idea about how to do it, too. (At least I thought I did.) I strode confidently into my bakery kitchen, fired up the oven, and began mixing away. I popped the cookies in the oven—and surprise! They didn't look or taste like the cookie I remembered. Oh well, they tasted good, so I sent them out to see if they would sell. Customers grabbed them up, exclaiming at how light they were, and how they had just the proper amount of sugar and crunch. By the end of the day, the cookies were gone. They were a mistake, but they sold like crazy. As the Christmas season approached, I realized my new cookie creations would make first-rate holiday presents. The small, sturdy meringues are perfect for stacking in cellophane bags. Tie them up with colorful ribbons and hand them out as party favors or hostess gifts.

Yield: About 2 dozen cookies

1 cup whole pecans

2 large egg whites

¾ cup sugar

½ teaspoon vanilla extract

1 cup sweetened shredded coconut

¼ cup sliced almonds

Preheat the oven to 350°F. Arrange the pecans on a rimmed baking sheet in a single layer and toast 7 to 9 minutes, until slightly darkened and aromatic. Remove from the oven and transfer to a bowl. Lower the oven temperature to 300°F. Let the pecans cool, then coarsely chop.

Line a baking sheet with parchment paper or a silicone mat. Using an electric mixer fitted with the whisk attachment, beat the egg whites on high speed until soft peaks form. (Make sure the bowl is perfectly free of grease, or the whites will not whip properly.) Slowly add the sugar, 1 tablespoon at a time, and continue beating until stiff glossy peaks form. Add the vanilla with the final tablespoon of sugar and beat until combined. Fold in the cooled pecans and coconut. Coarsely crush the almonds with your hands, then fold them into the cookie dough. Use a 1½-inch scoop to drop the cookies on the prepared pan. Bake for about 20 minutes, or until crunchy on the outside. The cookies will keep in an airtight container for 4 to 5 days.

RATHER SWEET VARIATION

Some people aren't happy unless there's a little chocolate in their cookie. Make their day by stirring in 1 cup mini chocolate chips with the nuts.

CHAPTER TWO

RANCH BARN BRUNCH

WHEN I NEED TO RELAX after a wild day at the bakery, I head to the hills and jump on my horse, Junior. He's more than seventeen hands tall, and he lives at my good friend and thoroughbred breeder Lane Hutchins's ranch. If I can't get to the ranch before sundown, just visiting Junior to stroke his velvet nose and talk softly to him melts away the stresses of the day. I spend as much time as I can at the barn. Naturally, I think of a ranch barn as a perfect party venue. With Fredericksburg's mild winters, an indoor-outdoor holiday party makes sense.

Jay and Patty Jones live in a beautifully decorated Texas-style home set among rolling hills dotted with Texas oaks. The party photographed in this chapter took place in their old cattle barn. Jay and Patty are veteran entertainers who moved to Fredericksburg about eight years ago. "We love to cook. People often ask us why we don't open up a restaurant," Jay says. His answer: "So we can do the dishes and go to bed." Outdoor cooking is Jay's specialty; he recently cooked a whole hog for his daughter's wedding rehearsal dinner. How'd he do it? "Very slowly," he says.

For Jay and Patty's Ranch Barn Brunch party, I used a lot of my Mexican pottery. I love the idea of using a colorful Mexican motif for a holiday party. Mexican tin candle holders are available nationwide at import stores. Or use whatever candle holders you have on hand and light plenty of candles. A host of tall tapers sets a party mood, and they can be purchased inexpensively at just about any grocery store. Use your imagination and whatever is already around the house for decorating. I've used bandanas for napkins and old shawls for table coverings. And I try to have a little something special at the table for each party guest. During the holidays it's a small ornament, a cookie cutter, or a Christmas "cracker."

When discussing plans for Jay and Patty's party, Jay suggested that I ride up to the barn on my horse, stop at his front gate, and let him hand me a cranberry margarita (page 52). This sounded like a great idea until I broke my arm a few weeks before the party. (No, it didn't happen on horseback, but while I was working in someone else's kitchen.) For the time being, all of my holiday drinks will be sipped at ground level.

Larry Doll's Famous Cranberry Margaritas

When my friend Margie heard I was writing a Christmas cookbook, she forwarded this recipe from her colleague, associate professor Larry Doll. His margaritas are served at the holiday parties held at the Charles Moore House for the University of Texas at Austin School of Architecture. Larry does not think that a salt rim is right with the cranberry. He suggests a section of fresh red grapefruit as a garnish. I favor a more traditional approach and use a thinly sliced round of lime. I agree that salted glasses would be a mistake, but you might try running a bit of cut lime round the rim and dipping it in sugar.

{ Yield: 4 servings }

¼ cup fresh lime juice

¼ cup orange liqueur (Triple Sec, Citronage, or Grand Marnier)

½ cup "vitamin T" (silver or other 100 percent agave tequila)

½ cup cranberry juice

Ice cubes for shaking and serving

4 thin slices lime for garnish

Combine the lime juice, liqueur, tequila, and cranberry juice in a cocktail shaker filled with ice and shake like hell. Pour into ice-filled jelly glasses. Garnish each glass with a lime slice and serve.

TIP: These go down easily, but be warned—they are very potent.

Texas Antipasto Platter

This platter includes some of my favorite party appetizers—Sea Salt Roasted Almonds, Shrimp Rémoulade, and Focaccia Bruschetta—served buffet style. Strictly speaking, the Shrimp Rémoulade is the only one with real Texas roots (I serve it frequently to showcase our state's succulent Gulf shrimp), but grouped together the trio makes for a hearty, larger-than-life spread that will satisfy a host of the hungriest partygoers. In my book, that's quintessential Texas eating.

Sea Salt Roasted Almonds

For simple, elegant cocktail fodder, oven-roasted almonds with a touch of smoked sea salt are tough to top. Set a few small bowls of these around the room and watch them disappear. Smoked sea salt can be found at specialty foods stores.

{ Yield: 8 servings }

2 cups whole blanched almonds
1 tablespoon extra-virgin olive oil
2 teaspoons smoked sea salt

Preheat the oven to 350°F. Line a baking sheet with aluminum foil. In a medium bowl, toss the almonds with olive oil, then the sea salt, until they are evenly coated. Arrange in a single layer on the prepared pan and bake for 12 to 15 minutes, until a deep golden brown. (A few minutes before the almonds are done, you will hear them crack.) Remove from the oven and let cool.

Shrimp Rémoulade

As children, we went on many a shrimping expedition at our summertime playground on the Bolivar Peninsula, a spit of land between Galveston Bay and the Gulf of Mexico. (It's still a fishing mecca for tourists and locals.) Shrimp rémoulade became one of my mother's signature party foods (see photo on page 59).

{ Yield: 8 servings }

1 cup mayonnaise (recipe follows, or use store-bought mayo)

3 tablespoons chili sauce

1 tablespoon sweet relish

2 teaspoons Creole mustard, or any whole-grain mustard

2 teaspoons prepared horseradish

1 inner stalk celery, finely chopped

1 green onion, including green parts, thinly sliced

4 cornichons, finely chopped

1 teaspoon hot Hungarian paprika

1 clove garlic, minced

¼ teaspoon kosher salt

2 pounds large shrimp, cooked, shelled, and deveined (see Tip)

In a small bowl, whisk together the mayonnaise, chili sauce, sweet relish, mustard, and horseradish. Stir in the celery, onion, cornichons, paprika, garlic, and salt. Cover and refrigerate for at least 30 minutes or up to 2 days. Serve as a dipping sauce with the cold shrimp.

TIP: You can buy ready-to-eat cooked shrimp at the grocery store, but if you'd like to cook the shrimp yourself, here's how: Buy frozen shelled and deveined large shrimp with the tails left on. (I get mine from my local warehouse store. Although cooking shrimp with the shell on gives them more flavor, I find shelling and deveining shrimp to be far too time-consuming.) Fill a large stockpot with water and add half an onion cut into quarters, 5 to 10 whole peppercorns, a bay leaf, a celery stalk cut into 4 pieces, and a few baby carrots. Bring the water to a boil, add the shrimp, and simmer for about 3 minutes, just until the shrimp turn pink. Drain and plunge them into a large bowl filled with ice water to stop them from cooking further. Once they are completely cooled, drain and pat the shrimp dry, store them in a plastic bag, and refrigerate for up to 1 day before serving.

Mayonnaise

{ Yield: 1½ cups }

2 large eggs

1 large egg yolk

1 teaspoon kosher salt

½ teaspoon freshly ground pepper

1 tablespoon Dijon mustard

2 tablespoons freshly squeezed lemon juice

1 cup canola oil

In a blender, process the eggs, egg yolk, salt, pepper, mustard, and lemon juice on medium speed until thoroughly mixed. Switch the blender to low speed and gradually add the oil in a slow, steady stream. The mayonnaise will thicken as you pour, taking on a creamy consistency just after all of the oil has been added. Pour into a clean container, cover, and refrigerate for up to 4 days.

Focaccia Bruschetta

We bake fresh focaccia daily for our signature sandwiches. One day, we ran out of the bread we use for making our in-house bruschetta, the traditional Italian appetizer. So I substituted sliced Rather Sweet focaccia. The change proved to be such a hit that I've been using it for parties, graduations, and receptions ever since. Focaccia is available in most grocery stores.

{ Yield: About 12 servings }

TOPPING

- 5 plum (Roma) tomatoes
- ½ cup pitted kalamata olives
- ½ cup packed fresh basil leaves
- 6 to 8 tablespoons high-quality extra-virgin olive oil
- 1½ tablespoons balsamic vinegar
- 1½ teaspoons minced garlic
- ½ teaspoon kosher salt

- 1 loaf focaccia bread
- 2 tablespoons salted butter, melted
- 2 tablespoons olive oil

To make the topping: Stem the tomatoes, cut them in half crosswise, scoop out the pulp and seeds and discard. Cut the tomatoes into ¼-inch pieces and put them in a medium bowl. Cut the kalamata olives in half lengthwise. Cut the basil leaves into slivers. Add the olives, basil, olive oil, vinegar, garlic, and salt to the tomatoes and stir until combined. Cover the bowl with plastic wrap and let stand at room temperature for 30 minutes to 1 hour.

Preheat the oven to 375°F. Cut the focaccia bread into ¼-inch-thick slices. In a small bowl, combine the melted butter and olive oil. Place the focaccia slices on a baking sheet and brush the tops with the butter mixture. Toast in the oven for 20 to 25 minutes, until golden brown. Serve the toasts stacked on a platter accompanied with bowls of the tomato mixture and let people create their own. (Make sure to provide little plates and plenty of napkins, because the process can get messy.)

TIP: The dictionary says bruschetta comes from the Italian word *bruscare*, meaning "to roast over coals." Today, most people use a grill or broiler to toast the bread. (Heck, you could even use a toaster.) In my version, instead of rubbing toasted bread slices with garlic, I add minced garlic to the tomato topping. I like my bruschetta very wet, with plenty of olive oil, so I use the maximum amount listed in the recipe. Experiment with varying amounts of olive oil and decide which version you like best.

TIP: If there happens to be tomato mixture left over, use it as an accompaniment to broiled fish, or transform it into a puttanesca-style sauce for pasta: In a large saucepan, sauté ½ cup diced onion in 1 tablespoon olive oil, add a 15-ounce can of peeled tomatoes (if you have more than a cup of tomato mixture left over, use a 28-ounce can), and stir in what is left of the tomato mixture. Add 1 tablespoon drained capers and a dash of minced fresh oregano and simmer for about 15 minutes. Serve over fresh-cooked pasta, or refrigerate to serve the next day.

Seasonal Fruit Salad with Poppy Seed Dressing

My mother just loved poppy seed dressing. It was one of the few festive things she could enjoy that complied with her no-salt diet. Whenever we ate lunch at Neiman Marcus, she'd order the fruit salad with poppy seed dressing. I like to make it with winter fruits that are slightly tart and not too juicy. A few chopped toasted nuts thrown in just before serving add a final crunchy touch.

{ **Yield: 4 servings** }

DRESSING

6 tablespoons sugar

½ teaspoon dry mustard

2 tablespoons plus 2 teaspoons white wine vinegar

1 tablespoon grated white onion

½ cup canola oil

1½ teaspoons poppy seeds

2 Granny Smith apples, cored and diced

2 Bosc pears, cored and diced

2 clementine or Satsuma oranges, peeled and sectioned

Seeds from 1 pomegranate

½ cup walnuts or pecans, toasted

To make the dressing: In an electric blender, blend the sugar, mustard, vinegar, and onion on medium-low speed. With the machine running, gradually add the oil. Add the poppy seeds and blend just to incorporate. Pour the dressing into a glass jar. Cover and refrigerate any leftover dressing for up to 1 week.

In a large bowl, toss the fruit with ½ cup of the dressing. Refrigerate for at least 30 minutes or up to 5 hours. Add the nuts just before serving and toss to mix.

Brown Sugar Bacon

Every morning, I am faced with a huge, fresh stack of crisp applewood smoked bacon ready to be mixed into our signature Apple-Smoked Bacon and Cheddar Scones. (For the recipe, see my first book, The Pastry Queen.) If I could stay away from it, I'll bet I could lose ten pounds. While bacon is good in almost everything, it is especially good when covered with a thin blanket of brown sugar and baked so the sugar caramelizes and surrounds each slice with a lovely sweet-salty coating. Make sure to use thick-sliced bacon, or it will be difficult to thread on skewers for serving. A natural dish to serve Christmas morning, Brown Sugar Bacon (see photo on page 63) can be assembled quickly the night before and baked while the family opens presents.

{ Yield: 6 servings }

One 12-ounce package thick-sliced bacon, preferably apple smoked

1 cup firmly packed golden brown sugar

Separate the bacon slices and lay them in one layer on a large baking sheet. Sprinkle brown sugar evenly over the bacon. Cover with aluminum foil or plastic wrap and refrigerate overnight.

Preheat the oven to 350°F. Coat a wire rack with cooking spray and set the rack on a piece of waxed or parchment paper; set aside.

Remove the foil or plastic wrap covering the bacon and bake until crisp, 25 to 30 minutes. Remove from the oven. Using tongs, transfer the bacon to the prepared wire rack. Let the slices cool to the touch, then cut them in half crosswise and thread the slices on a metal or wooden skewer. Arrange the skewers on a serving platter and serve the bacon at room temperature. For a less fussy approach, forget the skewers and just pile the bacon on a platter.

♛ **TIP:** I love Nueske's Applewood Smoked Bacon for this and any other recipe that calls for bacon. Call 800-392-2266, or visit their website at www.nueskes.com.

Cherry Tomatoes with Tequila-Lime Vinaigrette

I got the idea for tequila-bathed tomatoes from my friend Lucinda Hutson, an herbalist and author of The Herb Garden Cookbook. During my years in Austin, I spent many a happy moment in her wondrous garden. Lucinda was one of the original "pastry queens," a group of friends and food professionals who used to gather for monthly dinners. (I ended up with the title by being the only one who stuck with the pastry business. Being referred to in print as "the Pastry Queen" by an Austin food writer sealed the deal.) Lucinda knows how to throw a great party, with plenty of fabulous food and drink. This simple, refreshing salad will enhance any holiday buffet table.

{ Yield: 4 to 6 servings }

Juice of 1 lime

1 teaspoon sea salt

3 to 4 tablespoons tequila

1 teaspoon white wine vinegar

1 teaspoon minced fresh flat-leaf parsley

6 tablespoons olive oil

1 pint cherry tomatoes, sliced in half

In a medium bowl, whisk together the lime, salt, tequila, vinegar, parsley, and olive oil. Add the tomatoes and toss to coat. Let the tomatoes stand at room temperature for about 2 hours before serving.

Mexican Ranch Chilaquiles

Always dressed in a cowboy hat and boots, Jay Jones might be mistaken for a dressed-down Ralph Lauren, and his wife, Patty, is a fabulous Texas hostess. They are both consummate entertainers specializing in campfire and iron-pot cooking at their gorgeous ranch just outside of Fredericksburg. Patty makes a famously potent margarita, and Jay loves to cook using his extensive array of cast-iron pots. Chilaquiles have become a Jones family favorite. "All my kids love them, and the dish has become a Christmas morning tradition." Jay's outdoor fire pit and a recipe that easily triples mean Jay and Patty can stir up chilaquiles for crowds large and small. "I've done it for thirty people and used four dozen eggs," Jay says.

Chilaquiles are a Mexican specialty, originally created, I'm told, to use up stale corn tortillas that otherwise might be relegated to the trash. There are many variations, but the dish often includes eggs, tomatoes, cheese, green chiles, and tortillas, which soften and mellow as they soak up the liquid. Some even tout the dish as a hangover cure, though I wouldn't bet the ranch.

{ Yield: 6 servings }

TORTILLA STRIPS

1 package (8 to 10) corn tortillas

Peanut or canola oil for frying

2 tablespoons unsalted butter or olive oil

½ yellow onion, diced

1 poblano chile, seeded, deveined, and diced

1 clove garlic, minced

12 large eggs

½ teaspoon paprika

½ teaspoon freshly ground pepper

Dash of kosher salt

One 14-ounce can diced tomatoes and green chiles, drained

1½ cups (6 ounces) shredded sharp Cheddar cheese

1 plum (Roma) tomato, diced

½ cup fresh cilantro or flat-leaf parsley, stemmed

To make the tortilla strips: Using kitchen scissors, cut the corn tortillas into ¾-inch-wide strips. Heat ½ inch oil in a large sauté pan or Dutch oven over medium-high heat. The oil is ready when a piece of tortilla added to the oil turns light golden brown on one side in about 10 seconds. Using tongs, add the remaining strips in batches and fry for 8 to 10 seconds on each side, or until light golden brown and crisp. Transfer the strips to paper towels to drain. Use immediately, or store in an airtight container for up to 24 hours.

In a large sauté pan, melt 1 tablespoon butter (or heat 1 tablespoon oil) over medium heat. Add the onion and sauté until translucent, about 4 minutes. Stir in the poblano chile and garlic and sauté for another 2 minutes.

continued

Add the remaining tablespoon of butter or oil. In a medium bowl, whisk the eggs with the paprika, pepper, and salt. Pour the eggs into the heated skillet and stir until soft, taking care to loosen cooked bits of egg from the bottom and sides of the skillet. Stir in the canned tomatoes with chiles. Add the shredded cheese and stir until it melts completely. Stir in the tortilla strips. Top with the diced plum tomato arranged in the center and sprinkle with cilantro or parsley. Serve immediately. For an authentic cowboy look, serve the eggs directly from the skillet.

TIP: Homemade tortilla strips can be fun to make if you're not under time pressure. They quickly can become a burden when time is short. A 7- to 8-ounce bag of store-bought tortilla strips is a good substitute.

RATHER SWEET VARIATION

Meat lovers will appreciate the addition of chorizo sausage to this dish. Remove the casing from 1 pound of Mexican (fresh) chorizo, panfry it while breaking it up as it cooks, drain off the excess fat, and stir it into the egg mixture with the Cheddar cheese.

Pan de Campo
(Mexican Camp Bread)

Here's another recipe I picked up from Patty and Jay Jones, outdoor entertainers extraordinaire. Jay cooks this simple, versatile flat bread in a cast-iron pot or skillet set on an outdoor fire pit. You can just as easily cook it on top of your stove. "It's great with eggs, beans, stew, or gravy," Jay advises. Or cut it in half, spread it with refried beans and bacon, and eat it for breakfast. As Jay says, with gusto, "Easy, fun, fantastic—Mexican camp bread."

{ **Yield: 6 flat breads** }

4 cups all-purpose flour

2 tablespoons sugar

2 teaspoons baking powder

2 teaspoons kosher salt

6 tablespoons cold vegetable shortening

1½ cups buttermilk

6 tablespoons unsalted butter for frying

In a large bowl, combine the flour, sugar, baking powder, and salt. Use your hands or a pastry cutter to incorporate the shortening into the flour mixture until it is crumbly. Add the buttermilk ¾ cup at a time and lightly stir until just mixed.

Divide the dough into 6 equal portions and place on a lightly floured work surface. Gently roll each portion into a quarter-inch-thick disk about 6 inches in diameter.

Melt 1 tablespoon of the butter in a cast-iron or heavy bottomed skillet over medium heat. Add one of the disks and fry for 4 to 5 minutes on each side, until golden brown. (Use a metal spatula to flip the bread.) Repeat for the rest of the dough and serve immediately.

Leftovers can be wrapped in plastic wrap and reheated in a skillet or toaster to be enjoyed the next day.

Cast-Iron Skillet Potatoes

My mom loved to serve breakfast food for dinner. Often, she'd cook eggs and potatoes or steak and potatoes for nighttime meals. Skillet potatoes were one of her dinner specialties. I'm not big on eating breakfast at night, but I have mouthwatering memories of my mom's potatoes. I remember their wonderful flavor, and how Mom always added plenty of paprika, lending the potatoes an appealing reddish hue. I have substituted hot Hungarian paprika, which she didn't use, but I love the delicate heat it adds to the dish.

{ Yield: 6 to 8 servings }

3 to 4 tablespoons olive oil

1 yellow onion, sliced

¼ red onion, sliced

8 small red potatoes, quartered

6 Yukon Gold potatoes, cut into large dice

3 teaspoons kosher salt

½ teaspoon hot Hungarian paprika

½ to 1 teaspoon minced fresh rosemary

1 red bell pepper, seeded, deveined, and sliced

1 green bell pepper, seeded, deveined, and sliced

1 yellow banana pepper, seeded, deveined, and sliced (optional)

1 tablespoon minced garlic (about 3 cloves)

Kosher or sea salt to taste

½ teaspoon freshly ground pepper

TIP: Peppers add a lively touch of color to this dish, so I always try to use both red and green varieties. Beyond that, any pepper variety will do, so use your favorites. If spicy food is your thing, add as many hot peppers, such as jalapeños or serranos, as you can stand.

RATHER SWEET VARIATION

Reduce the olive oil to 2 tablespoons and add 8 ounces diced pancetta to the skillet with the onions and potatoes. The pancetta adds a salty flavor, so be sure to taste the potatoes before adding salt. Continue to cook as directed above.

In a large cast-iron or other heavy skillet, heat the olive oil over medium-high heat. Add the onions and potatoes, sprinkle with the salt and paprika, and sauté, stirring occasionally, until the onions brown and the potatoes begin to soften, 25 to 35 minutes. Add the rosemary, peppers, and garlic and continue sautéing until the potatoes are tender. Season with salt and pepper. Serve warm or at room temperature, directly from the skillet.

Apple-Spice Layer Cake with Caramel Swirl Icing

Here's a cake that showcases the flavors and smells of Christmas. This three-layer extravaganza has a touch of molasses and shredded apple to keep it moist. As the cake bakes, it fills the house with a fragrance that beats the most expensive holiday-scented candle.

Many amateur cooks are intimidated by just thinking about making a cake that doesn't come from a box. Yes, it takes extra time, but it isn't hard. Just follow the steps outlined below. I say, if you want to make an impression, bring on a tall, showy homemade cake. Your friends will be talking about it long after the party is over.

{ Yield: 12 to 14 servings }

1½ cups (3 sticks) unsalted butter at room temperature

3 cups sugar

2 tablespoons light molasses

6 large eggs

3 cups cake flour

1¼ teaspoons baking soda

¼ teaspoon kosher salt

2 tablespoons ground cinnamon

2 teaspoons ground allspice

1 teaspoon ground nutmeg

1 teaspoon ground ginger

1 cup sour cream

3 Granny Smith apples, peeled and shredded (about 1½ cups)

1 tablespoon vanilla extract

1 tablespoon grated fresh ginger (optional)

ICING

One 14-ounce bag caramels

4 tablespoons heavy whipping cream

2 tablespoons plus 1½ cups (3 sticks) unsalted butter at room temperature

1 teaspoon vanilla extract

3 cups powdered sugar

1 cup (8 ounces) mascarpone (Italian cream cheese, available at most grocery stores)

2 cups pecan pieces, toasted (optional)

Place one oven rack in the bottom third of the oven and a second rack in the top third of the oven. Preheat the oven to 350°F. Grease three 9-inch cake pans with butter or cooking spray, then line each with a parchment paper round and grease the rounds.

Using an electric mixer fitted with the paddle attachment, cream the butter and sugar on medium-high speed until light and fluffy, about 3 minutes. Scrape down the sides of the bowl with a rubber spatula. Beat in the molasses. Add the eggs, one at a time, beating between each addition. In a medium bowl, stir together the flour, baking soda, salt, and ground spices to blend. Add the flour mixture and sour cream alternately to the batter. (Start

continued

72

and end with the flour mixture, adding the flour mixture in 3 increments and the sour cream in 2 increments.) After each addition, mix on low speed just to combine the ingredients. Stir in the shredded apples, vanilla, and ginger.

Spoon the batter (it will be thick) evenly into the prepared pans. Place two cake pans side by side on one rack and the third on the other. Stagger the cake layers on the oven racks so that no layer is directly over another. Bake for 35 to 40 minutes, until firm to the touch. Monitor the layers carefully for doneness; each one may be done at a different time. Remove from the oven and let cool in the pans for 10 minutes. Run a knife around the edges of the pans and unmold the cakes onto wire racks to cool completely, 15 to 30 minutes, before frosting.

The cakes can be kept frozen, tightly wrapped in plastic wrap, for up to 3 weeks. Defrost them at room temperature before unwrapping. Frost immediately.

To make the icing: In a medium stainless-steel bowl, combine the unwrapped caramels, 2 tablespoons of the cream, and the 2 tablespoons butter. Place over a saucepan filled with 2 inches of simmering water. Stir the caramel mixture until smooth. Remove the bowl from the heat. Let cool, stirring the mixture every few minutes until cool to the touch, about 20 minutes. (If the mixture is too warm, it will melt the buttercream frosting when it is stirred in later.)

While the caramel is cooling, make the buttercream: Using an electric mixer fitted with the paddle attachment, beat the 1½ cups butter on medium-high speed for about 1 minute, until pale in color. Add the remaining 2 tablespoons cream and the vanilla and powdered sugar, and beat for 3 minutes, until light and fluffy. Add the mascarpone and beat on medium-low speed until incorporated. Do not overbeat the mascarpone, or it may separate. Reserve ¼ cup of the cooled caramel mixture to drizzle over the cake once it is frosted. Stir the remainder of the caramel into the frosting, using large strokes to create caramel swirls throughout. Don't stir it too much or the ribbons of caramel will disappear.

Place one cake layer on a serving plate and spread a thick blanket of frosting on top. Add the second layer and spread thickly with frosting. Add the third layer and cover the top and sides of the cake with an even layer of frosting. Use a small spoon to drizzle the reserved ¼ cup of caramel over the top of the cake. Pat on the toasted pecan pieces to cover the sides of the cake.

TIP: Using the proper tools for cutting frosted layer cakes ensures that individual servings look as good as they taste. I use a large serrated knife dipped in hot water for cutting. I wipe the knife off with a clean dishcloth after each piece, which ensures that every cut is as clean as the first.

Earthquake Cake

The inspiration for my Earthquake Cake came from Chocolatier magazine's Cocoa Blackout Cake, which appeared in their Glorious Chocolate: The Ultimate Chocolate Cookbook. I used my own recipe for the cake and adapted Chocolatier's recipe for the frosting. When I was an executive pastry chef for a national chain of cafés, people would come into the store and request "that natural disaster cake." They never could get it right. "You know," they'd say, "the cyclone cake, tornado cake, hurricane cake, whatever."

Names aside, this cake is supposed to look like a disaster. The third layer of cake is cut into varying shapes and the pieces are stuck all over the frosted two-layer cake. Don't let your inner perfectionist make it too neat, even, or orderly (a common mistake). Go for wild, jagged, and uneven. You know, like an earthquake.

{ Yield: 12 to 14 servings }

1 cup (2 sticks) unsalted butter

2 cups water

1 cup canola oil

4 cups granulated sugar

1 cup high-quality unsweetened cocoa powder

4 cups all-purpose flour

4 large eggs

1 cup buttermilk

1 tablespoon vanilla extract

1 tablespoon baking soda

½ teaspoon kosher salt

FROSTING

2 cups heavy whipping cream

4 tablespoons unsalted butter

1 vanilla bean, split lengthwise

2 cups granulated sugar

2 cups unsweetened cocoa powder

½ teaspoon kosher salt

¼ cup Lyle's Golden Syrup or light corn syrup

¼ cup powdered sugar for dusting

Place an oven rack in the bottom third of the oven and another rack in the upper third of the oven. Preheat the oven to 350°F. Grease three 9-inch cake pans with butter and then line each with a parchment paper round. Butter the paper, then dust the pan with flour and knock out the excess (or spray with Baker's Joy).

In a medium saucepan, combine the butter, water, and oil and cook over medium heat until the butter is melted. In a large bowl, stir together the granulated sugar, cocoa powder, and flour. Pour the butter mixture into the sugar mixture and whisk until smooth.

Whisk in the eggs, one at a time, then whisk in the buttermilk and vanilla. Whisk in the baking soda and salt. Spoon the batter evenly into the prepared pans. Place two layers on the top rack and the third on the lower rack. Stagger the cake layers on the oven racks so that no

continued

layer is directly over another. Bake for 35 to 40 minutes, until a toothpick inserted in the middle of each layer comes out clean. Monitor the layers carefully for doneness; each one may be done at a different time.

Remove the layers from the oven and let cool in the pans on wire racks for about 15 minutes before unmolding onto the racks. Let cool completely, at least 2 hours, before frosting.

To make the frosting: In a large saucepan, combine the cream, butter, and vanilla bean, and stir until the butter is melted. Remove the vanilla bean and whisk in the granulated sugar, cocoa powder, salt, and syrup until smooth (this will take about 5 minutes). Pour into a 9 by 13-inch pan and freeze until firm, about 2 hours, or refrigerate for at least 8 hours or overnight.

Remove the frosting from the freezer or refrigerator. Using an electric mixer fitted with the paddle attachment, beat the frosting on medium speed for about 2 minutes. (For the first few minutes, the frosting is too stiff for the whisk attachment to handle.) Change to the whisk attachment and beat at medium-high speed until the frosting is light and fluffy, about 5 minutes.

To assemble the cake: Remove the parchment paper from the bottom of the cake layers. Spread one-third of the frosting over the top of the first layer. Set the second layer on top and use the remainder of the frosting to cover the top and sides. Slice the third layer horizontally into 2 even layers. Cut each layer into strips of varying widths, though not narrower than 1 inch nor wider than 2 inches. Cut each strip into a mix of squares, triangles, and rectangles. Press the cake pieces into the top and on the sides of the frosted cake until

the entire surface is covered. Use a sieve to lightly dust the cake with an even coating of powdered sugar.

TIP: The unfrosted cake can be made in advance. Well wrapped, it can be refrigerated for up to 3 days or frozen for up to 1 month. Defrost the cake layers at room temperature for about 2 hours, then remove the wrapping and frost.

Cowboy Cookies

Childhood food memories are among the most vivid. I finally got the recipe for these cookies after my friend Doug repeatedly described them as his absolute favorites. He remembered eating them by the plateful at a Colorado dude ranch where he worked as a teenager. It turns out the ranch is still going strong, and the owners happily gave me the recipe, which appears in their self-published cookbook, The Deer Valley Ranch Cookbook. Doug insists these are the best ever, and my customers seem to agree. The Deer Valley recipe calls for nuts, but I leave them out for several of my customers who hate them. They are one of the few nut-free cookies I make.

{ Yield: About 4 dozen cookies }

1 cup (2 sticks) unsalted butter at room temperature

1 cup firmly packed brown sugar

1 cup granulated sugar

2 large eggs

1 teaspoon vanilla extract

2 cups all-purpose flour

1 teaspoon baking soda

½ teaspoon baking powder

½ teaspoon kosher salt

2 cups old-fashioned rolled oats

One 12-ounce package chocolate chips

Preheat the oven to 350°F. Line baking sheets with parchment paper or silicone mats, or grease generously with butter or cooking spray. Using an electric mixer fitted with the paddle attachment, beat the butter and sugars on medium speed until light and fluffy, about 1 minute. Scrape down the sides with a rubber spatula, add the eggs and vanilla, and beat on medium speed for about 1 minute more. In a medium bowl, stir together the flour, baking soda, baking powder, salt, and oats. Add the flour mixture all at once to the butter mixture and beat on low speed until incorporated.

The dough will be stiff. Stir in the chocolate chips.

Using a 1½-inch-diameter ice cream scoop to make large cookies, drop the dough 2 inches apart onto the prepared pans. Bake for 10 to 12 minutes, until golden brown. (When cool, the cookies should be chewy in the middle.)

RATHER SWEET VARIATION

I often add 1½ cups of dried cranberries to this recipe along with the chocolate chips.

Bite-Sized Sticky Buns

As soon as I tried Martha's Best-Ever Rolls (page 114), I imagined using the dough to make sticky buns. I had a hunch that these soft, fluffy yeast rolls would make the perfect base for a blanket of warm caramel syrup. I tested the idea soon afterward, and the result was as delicious as I'd hoped. After making the sticky buns, you'll have enough leftover dough to fill two greased 9-inch cake pans with seven rolls apiece. Wrap them well and freeze them in the pans for up to 1 month, or let them rise, bake, and serve for dinner.

Advance planning is needed for this recipe, as the dough must be made a day ahead and refrigerated overnight. But the dough keeps, and once it is placed with the caramel syrup in muffin tins, it can be refrigerated for up to 3 days. Let the buns rise at room temperature and bake them just before serving. For a very special Christmas gift, wrap a muffin pan filled with unbaked sticky buns and attach a tag with baking instructions. Your friends will love you for it.

{ Yield: 2 dozen sticky buns }

1 cup whole pecans

½ cup (1 stick) unsalted butter

1½ cups firmly packed brown sugar

½ cup Lyle's Golden Syrup or light corn syrup

Pinch of kosher salt

Dough for Martha's Best-Ever Rolls (page 114), made through the second stage

Preheat the oven to 350°F. Arrange the pecans in a single layer on a baking sheet and toast for 7 to 9 minutes, until darker in color and aromatic. Remove from the oven and allow them to cool.

Turn the oven to 400°F. In a medium saucepan, combine the butter, brown sugar, syrup, and salt. Cook over medium heat until the butter and sugar are melted and bubbly. Coarsely chop the pecans. Grease standard muffin pans with butter or cooking spray. Place 2 tablespoons of the syrup mixture in each muffin cup (there will be syrup left over for drizzling over the cooked sticky buns) and sprinkle with pecans.

Using a sharp knife, cut off pieces of dough about the size of golf balls. Place a dough ball in each muffin cup. Let rise in a warm place until the dough is about 1 inch above the top of the pan (this may take up to 1 hour, depending on the warmth of your kitchen).

Bake for 15 to 20 minutes, until golden brown. Remove from the oven and immediately unmold onto a platter or large plate. (The caramel will be on top and will drip down the sides of each bun.) Drizzle more caramel syrup over the tops and sides of the muffins, if desired. Serve warm or at room temperature.

RATHER SWEET VARIATION

Substitute chopped toasted walnuts or slivered almonds for the pecans.

Sopaipillas

Another winning recipe from the Deer Valley Ranch, a dude ranch in the Colorado Rockies west of Colorado Springs. Every summer, guests and wranglers alike gobble up Sue DeWalt's sopaipillas in large numbers. Recipes abound for this Southwestern treat, but this is one of my favorites. The sopaipilla dough is deep-fried, which transforms it into puffy, golden brown pillows with hollow centers. Commonly eaten slathered with soft butter and warm honey, sopaipillas are also delicious stuffed with chili, meat, beans, or cheese.

{ Yield: About 2 dozen }

¼ cup warm (110° to 115°F) water

1 package active dry yeast

1 large egg, beaten

½ cup dry nonfat milk whisked with
   1½ cups warm water

⅓ cup unsalted butter, melted

⅓ cup sugar

1 teaspoon kosher salt

4 cups all-purpose flour

4 cups vegetable oil for deep-frying, such
   as canola or safflower

Butter, honey, and powdered sugar for
   serving

In a large bowl, stir together the water and yeast until the yeast dissolves. Let stand until foamy, about 5 minutes. Whisk in the egg, milk mixture, butter, sugar, salt, and 2 cups of the flour. Put the dough in a large oiled bowl, turn to coat, cover with a damp cloth, and let stand in a warm place until doubled in size, about 1 hour.

Stir in the remaining 2 cups flour. Knead the dough in the bowl for about 1 minute, until it forms a soft dough. Cover and let rise in a warm place until doubled in bulk, about 1 hour. Punch down and use now, or cover and refrigerate for up to 2 days. On a floured work surface, roll out the dough to a ⅛-inch thickness. Cut into 4-inch triangles or squares.

In a large, heavy sauté pan or Dutch oven, heat the oil over medium heat until it reaches 365°F on a candy thermometer. The oil is ready when a small piece of dough dropped into it sinks to the bottom, then rises to the top immediately. Fry the pieces of dough in batches just until they are puffy and golden brown. They will rise to the top and then turn themselves over. Using a wire skimmer, transfer to paper towels to drain. Serve immediately with butter, honey, and a dusting of powdered sugar.

Cowboy Coffee Straight

With all the newfangled, complicated coffee-making gadgets on the market today, it's easy to forget the old-fashioned cowboy way of brewing coffee. (What could be more Texas?) Dump the grounds in a coffee pot, let it sit overnight, and heat it over the campfire (or stove). It may not be the fanciest, but it works. Add a dollop of whiskey-kissed whipped cream, and you've got a virtual cowboy heaven on earth.

{ **Yield: 12 servings** }

12 cups cool water, plus 1 cup boiling

1 cup ground coffee of your choice

WHISKEY-KISSED WHIPPED CREAM

½ cup heavy whipping cream

¼ cup powdered sugar

1 tablespoon Bushmills Irish whiskey

Pour the 12 cups of water into a coffeepot. Add the ground coffee. Let the mixture stand overnight. (Do not refrigerate.) Heat the coffeepot over the fire or stove until the liquid simmers. Add the 1 cup of boiling water to settle the grounds

To make the whiskey-kissed whipped cream: Using an electric mixer fitted with the whisk attachment, beat the cream on medium-high speed until soft peaks form. Beat in the powdered sugar and whiskey.

Pour the hot coffee into mugs and top each serving with a dollop of flavored whipped cream.

RATHER SWEET VARIATIONS

To make Double-Whiskey Cowboy Coffee, fill mugs three-fourths full with hot coffee. Add 1 shot Bushmills Irish whiskey and a heaping tablespoonful of whiskey-kissed whipped cream to each cup. Serve immediately.

Native Texans Patty and Jay Jones have perfected the art of brewing cowboy coffee using Jay's campfire coffeepots. They recommend other potent coffee additions, including Baileys Irish Cream and a shot of fine tequila. On hunting trips, they warm up with coffee and Controy (a Mexican version of the orange-flavored liqueur Cointreau). "It's unique and very South Texas," Patty says.

Making Gingerbread Houses

When Tiffany & Company calls, for whatever reason, it's hard to say no. That's how I got roped into one of the biggest construction projects of my life: making two 2 by 3-foot gingerbread replicas of the famous jewelry purveyors' flagship store in New York City. One gingerbread house was for display at Tiffany's new store in San Antonio, and the second was slated for a charity auction. I had already decided to include a gingerbread house–making section in this book, and figured the Tiffany project would be a good dry run. After spending an inordinate amount of time tinting royal icing to create a perfect match for the elegant Tiffany blue, I baked huge slabs of gingerbread that would become the multistory edifice. Once the houses were complete, I had to get the towering buildings to San Antonio, sixty miles away, a white-knuckle trip that involved equal parts fear and laughter (for comic relief). You should have seen the look on the faces of the Tiffany security guys when I tried to lug the things through the jewelry store's back door.

My Gingerbread Texas Hill Country Cabin is a much smaller affair. The pattern is loosely based on the weekend "Sunday houses" built by early Fredericksburg settlers so they could attend Sunday church and be spared a long horse-and-buggy trek to their farms outside of town. Originally one- or two-room affairs with porches, a few Sunday houses still stand, although they since have been transformed into small single-family homes.

This project is a multiday endeavor, so give yourself plenty of time. You'll need 6 batches of this dough to make the gingerbread cabin pictured opposite and on page 90. Each batch is large, so unless you have a commercial-style Hobart mixer, you'll be able to make only one batch at a time. (An electric mixer or high-powered food processor is a must for this project.)

Before you start baking, use the templates on pages 208–213 as a guide to make foam-board patterns for each of the cabin's components. (An Exacto knife makes cutting foam board a snap.) As soon as the gingerbread comes out of the oven, lay the patterns on top and cut them out using a sharp knife. Unless you live in a humid climate, the dough will stay hard indefinitely after it's cooled. For those who live in humid areas, wrap each piece with plastic or aluminum foil and freeze until all of the pieces are baked and ready for construction.

Many gingerbread houses are glued together with royal icing, a tried-and-true method that works well but takes a relatively long time to dry. I prefer to use sugar syrup that has been cooked to the hard-ball stage for constructing gingerbread houses. It hardens very quickly, saving you from holding walls together for minutes at a time while the royal icing hardens. Use the sugar syrup method with great care; the syrup is very hot and can cause painful burns if it drips on bare skin. Wear a long-sleeved shirt and have a bowl of ice water and some aloe vera on hand in case you get splattered. If you prefer, substitute 2 batches royal icing for the sugar-syrup glue and follow the directions below, holding each piece in place for 3 to 5 minutes, until the royal icing begins to harden. You'll need at least 4 batches of icing to cover the cabin and cabin base, with plenty left over for gluing on candy and piping decorations.

Decorating gingerbread houses is more fun in groups. Why not throw a party? Whip up a dinner that allows people to help themselves, and find out just how creative your friends can be. Sour Cream and Chicken Enchiladas (page 92) can be made ahead and baked just before your guests arrive. Serve them with Guacamole with Pico de Gallo (page 93) and a make-ahead dessert such as Torched S'mores (page 94) or Chocolate-Dipped Peanut Butter Sandwich Bites (page 96).

The gingerbread recipe (opposite) was adapted from a 1969 book called *The Cooking of Germany,* by Nika Standen Hazelton and the editors of Time-Life Books. It makes a very hard and durable gingerbread that will last for years in a cool, dry climate.

You'll find a list of suggested candies for decorating, but half the fun is discovering your own decorative materials. Walk through the bulk-foods section of your local natural foods store for inspiration, and don't overlook the wide array of nuts and seeds. Many pastry chefs use hot poured sugar to make windows, a tricky endeavor. I've discovered that sheets of gelatin, available at many specialty baking stores and on the web at www.kitchenkrafts. com, look great and are easy to work with.

You will need:

Exacto knife to cut out foam-board pattern pieces
Foam board to make pattern pieces (see pages 208–213 for measurements)
One 22 by 24-inch foam-board base
6 batches Gingerbread dough (recipe opposite)
4 batches Royal Icing (recipe opposite)

Gingerbread House

GINGERBREAD

¾ cup honey

1¾ cups sugar

¼ cup (½ stick) unsalted butter

⅓ cup freshly squeezed lemon juice

6¼ cups all-purpose flour

6 tablespoons baking powder

1½ teaspoons ground cinnamon

1 teaspoon ground cloves

¼ teaspoon ground nutmeg

¼ teaspoon ground cardamom

⅛ teaspoon kosher salt

1 large egg

1 large egg yolk

SUGAR SYRUP GLUE

2 cups sugar

Water as needed

ROYAL ICING

4 large egg whites

5 cups powdered sugar

Food coloring of your choice

SUGGESTED CANDY AND MATERIALS FOR DECORATING:

Chocolate rocks

Rock candy

White candy-coated chocolate-mint balls

Swedish ribbon candy

Pumpkin seed brittle (for the chimney)

Fruit leather (for window shutters)

Assorted hard candy and jelly beans

Assorted dragées and colored sprinkles

Candy canes or biscotti (for porch posts)

Maple sugar candy people

Gelatin sheets (for windows)

Unsweetened or sweetened flaked coconut (for snow)

TO MAKE THE GINGERBREAD: Preheat the oven to 375°F. Grease a 12 by 17-inch rimmed baking sheet with Baker's Joy, or line it with parchment paper. In a large saucepan, combine the honey, sugar, and butter and bring to a boil over high heat. Cook, stirring occasionally, until the sugar dissolves and the butter is melted. Remove from the heat and stir in the lemon juice. Transfer the mixture to the large bowl of an electric mixer.

In a separate large bowl, stir together the flour, baking powder, cinnamon, cloves, nutmeg, cardamom, and salt. Using an electric mixer fitted with the paddle attachment, beat 2 cups of the flour mixture into the cooled honey mixture at medium speed. Add the egg and egg yolk and beat on medium speed until combined, then add the remaining flour mixture and beat until the flour is thoroughly incorporated and the dough is smooth. (If you have a large heavy-duty food processor, you can also mix the dough in it, following the directions above.)

Immediately press the dough evenly into the prepared pan, then use a lightly floured rolling pin to smooth and even it out. (Do not let the dough sit after mixing, or it will be difficult to work into the baking sheet.) Bake for about 35 minutes, until firm and browned. Place a large cutting board on top of the gingerbread and flip it over to unmold. Place foam-board templates on top of the gingerbread and use them as guides to cut out the cabin pieces (including windows). The gingerbread must be cut warm from the oven, or it will harden and become almost impossible to cut.

Repeat to make and cut out 5 more batches of gingerbread, for a total of 6 batches. Do not start building the cabin until you have made all of the component pieces.

GETTING STARTED: Have the 22 by 24-inch foam-board base and all the gingerbread pieces lined up and ready. Hold the pieces in place to make sure you understand how they fit together. Read through all the following steps now, before you do anything else.

TO MAKE THE SUGAR SYRUP GLUE: Pour the sugar into a heavy 12-inch skillet and add water just to cover. Bring the mixture to a boil over medium-high heat and cook until it reaches the hard-ball stage on a candy thermometer (250° to 265°F). To keep the sugar glue from hardening, reduce the heat to medium-low while you work.

TO BUILD THE CABIN:
Walls: Attach front wall W1 to side wall W2, making a square corner. To do this, dip one of the connecting edges in sugar glue (careful—it's hot!), then quickly align the edges and hold them together for about 30 seconds, until glue sets. (Note: At the corner, set the edge of W2 inside W1 to hide the wall joint from the front.) Attach back wall W3 to W2 (again setting the side wall inside the back wall). Dip both short edges of W4 in the sugar glue, then set in place to complete the cabin walls. Center the walls on the B1 gingerbread base and attach the walls to the base.

Roof: Dip the short ends of roof panels R1 and R2 in the sugar glue and set the panels squarely on the wall tops.

Chimney: Attach chimney sides C2 and C3 to chimney back C1, gluing the long edges. Align C4 with the chimney top, roof notch down. Attach the chimney to the cabin side, matching the notch to the roof.

Eave supports: Attach triangular supports S1–S8 to the four walls, two per side, with their long edges vertical and the top corners aligned to the wall tops, about 1 inch in from the wall edges.

Eaves: Spoon sugar glue onto the top edges of S1 and S2, then join the long edges of E1 and W1 and set E1 onto its supports to form the front eave. Spoon sugar glue onto the long joined edge for added strength. Repeat for eaves E2–E5.

Porch posts: Attach porch posts P1–P4 vertically, just under the eave corners. Or, use 6-inch candy canes or biscotti for porch posts. (If the porch posts are short, cut small squares of fruit leather and stack them beneath each post as needed to increase the posts' height.)

The cabin's done—time to decorate.

TO MAKE THE ROYAL ICING: Using an electric mixer fitted with the whisk attachment, beat the egg whites on high speed until foamy, about 1 minute. Add the powdered sugar 1 cup at a time, beating on medium speed to combine after each addition. Increase the speed to high and beat for 5 minutes, or until the icing becomes thick and glossy. To keep the icing from drying out, keep it covered at all times with a clean, damp dish towel.

Make 1 or 2 batches of icing to start, then see how far it goes as you begin to decorate. The icing will keep for up to 12 hours covered with a damp towel. Making a batch of icing is relatively fast, so it's best to make only as much as you need at a given time.

TO PREPARE THE FOAM BOARD: Set the foam board atop 4 wood blocks at the corners. (This will make it easier to decorate the edges of the foam board.) Using a large spatula, cover the foam-board base with royal icing, then transfer the gingerbread cabin (and gingerbread base) to the center of the freshly iced foam-board base to hold the structure securely in place.

TO INSTALL THE WINDOWS: Using an Exacto knife, cut gelatin windowpanes about ½ inch wider around the edges than the window openings. Using a pastry bag fitted with a small tube, squeeze a line of royal icing around the window's edges. Press the window in place on the exterior wall and hold until the icing sets. Using fruit leather, cut custom shutters and affix them with royal icing.

TO DECORATE WITH ROYAL ICING: Tint separate batches of icing with any colors you wish for painting and decorating your gingerbread cabin. I used a small amount of black food coloring to create a gray color for the cabin's exterior, as many of the Sunday houses featured tin roofs and stone walls. (A cheap, clean, pocket-sized comb makes lifelike roof striations.) Pure royal icing piped on with a small round tip made the white lines on the exterior walls, and green piped icing made contrasting roof decorations. Use piped-on royal icing to glue on candy decorations. Thin royal icing with a few tablespoons of water and spoon it over the chimney and roof to mimic snow drifts.

HOW LONG WILL IT LAST? That depends on your location. Food stylist and friend Erica McNeish still has gingerbread houses she made years ago with the same gingerbread recipe used here. She wrapped her house in a plastic bag and stored it in a plastic bin. She lives in Denver, a low-humidity city.

Here in high-humidity Texas, gingerbread houses will not have the same lasting power. Mine started to soften about a week after it was completed. For some, that's a signal to start munching away. Those bent on saving their work longer will have to forgo any thought of eating it. Use lacquer spray to cover the gingerbread pieces before putting them together. Decorate with royal icing and candy as described above and spray it again, and your gingerbread creation will likely keep until next Christmas.

Sour Cream and Chicken Enchiladas

This is a very kid-friendly dish. My teenage friend Graham Comstock barely eats, but when I served this, he had a double portion. This can be made ahead, covered, and refrigerated unbaked for up to two days. It's a great addition to a holiday buffet.

Yield: 6 to 8 servings

1 store-bought roasted chicken
  (3 to 4 pounds)

4 tablespoons (½ stick) unsalted butter

1 large yellow onion, chopped

8 ounces button or cremini mushrooms,
  sliced (optional)

2 cloves garlic, minced

4 cups (32 ounces) sour cream

½ cup heavy whipping cream

One 7-ounce can diced green chiles,
  undrained

One 10-ounce can tomatoes with green
  chiles

¼ teaspoon kosher salt

¼ teaspoon freshly ground pepper

1 cup fresh or frozen corn kernels (about
  3 ears), or one 8-ounce can corn kernels

1 cup canola oil

12 corn tortillas

2½ cups (10 ounces) shredded Monterey
  jack cheese

Preheat the oven to 350°F. Grease a 9 by 13-inch baking pan with butter or cooking spray.

Remove and discard the skin from the cooked chicken. Pull the meat from the bones, shred it into bite-sized pieces, and set it aside in a large bowl.

In a large skillet, melt the butter over medium heat. Add the onion, mushrooms, and garlic and sauté until the onion is translucent, about 4 minutes. Stir in the sour cream, heavy cream, green chiles, tomatoes, salt, and pepper until smooth. Cook until warmed through, being careful not to let the mixture boil. Reserve 2 cups of the sour cream mixture for pouring over the casserole. Stir the corn and chicken into the remaining sour cream mixture, which will be used to fill the tortillas.

In a large skillet, heat the canola oil over medium-high heat. Using metal tongs, dip each tortilla in the hot oil for a few seconds on each side, until softened. Stack the tortillas on a paper towel. Spoon a generous line of the chicken mixture down the center of each tortilla, roll it up, and place it, seam side down, in the prepared pan. Pour the reserved sour cream mixture evenly over the tortillas and sprinkle with the shredded cheese. Bake, uncovered, for 20 to 25 minutes, until the sauce bubbles and the cheese is melted. Serve immediately.

RATHER SWEET VARIATIONS

Add a line of cooked, drained spinach (a 10-ounce package of frozen spinach will do) on top of the chicken mixture before rolling the tortillas. You also may substitute white or whole-wheat tortillas for corn tortillas, but don't dip them in hot oil to soften. Just fill them with the chicken mixture, roll them up, and place them in the casserole, seam side down.

For a lower-fat version of this dish, use non-fat or reduced-fat sour cream, omit the heavy whipping cream, and dip the tortillas in ½ cup chicken stock to soften them before filling.

(Add the chicken stock left over from dipping to the sour cream sauce.) The tortillas may split somewhat, but it won't show once they are covered in the sour cream sauce.

Guacamole with Pico de Gallo

Guacamole is my favorite food. I could eat it every day, although it is not always in my diet plan. Sometimes I even think about having guacamole and chips for dinner, period. My guacamole is very basic, and that's the way I like it. I love avocados, and I don't want to mess with them too much. I often accompany guacamole with this simple pico de gallo. If you are expecting a large crowd, both recipes can be doubled easily.

Yield: 4 to 6 servings

3 to 4 ripe Hass avocados, halved and pitted

2 to 3 tablespoons freshly squeezed lime juice

1½ teaspoons kosher salt

3 tablespoons finely chopped red onion

2 plum (Roma) tomatoes, seeded and finely chopped

1 clove garlic, minced

Few drops Tabasco sauce or hot sauce of your choice

PICO DE GALLO

4 plum (Roma) tomatoes, seeded and diced

½ jalapeño pepper, seeded and minced

¼ red onion, diced

¼ cup minced fresh cilantro or flat-leaf parsley

Juice of 2 limes

½ teaspoon kosher salt

1 to 2 garlic cloves, minced

¼ teaspoon ground white pepper

Scoop the avocado flesh into a medium bowl. Mash the avocado with a potato masher and stir in the lime juice, salt, red onion, tomatoes, garlic, and Tabasco. Serve immediately, or cover tightly with plastic wrap (so no air comes between the plastic wrap and the guacamole) and refrigerate for up to 4 hours.

To make the pico de gallo: In a medium bowl, combine the tomatoes, jalapeño, onion, cilantro or parsley, lime juice, salt, garlic, and white pepper. Cover and refrigerate for at least 15 minutes or up to 4 days.

♕ **TIP:** We make our own chips at the bakery, and you can, too. In a large sauté pan or Dutch oven, heat 3 inches of canola oil over medium heat until it reaches 365°F on a candy thermometer. Using kitchen scissors, cut corn tortillas into quarters. Fry the tortillas in batches until golden and drain on paper towels. Salt to taste and serve.

♕ **TIP:** My mother taught me that burying an avocado pit in the guacamole will keep it from turning brown. Just before serving, I remove the pit.

Torched S'mores

Most people think of s'mores as a kids' dessert, but mention them and many adults talk longingly of their youthful s'more-eating days. Here, I've created a plated dessert with custom touches for each age group. There is a G-rated version for kids and an R-rated one for adults who like their chocolate with a liquor kick. The dessert starts with a graham cracker crust that is topped with a thick and gooey marshmallow layer. Then, I use my kitchen torch to give the marshmallow topping a golden brown, just-off-the-campfire look. Finally, I pour on a bittersweet chocolate sauce that should wipe out nostalgic memories of melted Hershey bars for good.

Yield: 16 bars

CRUST

- 4 cups graham cracker crumbs (about 32 crackers)
- ¼ cup powdered sugar
- 1¼ cups (2½ sticks) unsalted butter, melted
- 1 cup sliced almonds, toasted and lightly crushed

TOPPING

- 1½ envelopes (1½ tablespoons) unflavored gelatin
- 1 cup cold water
- 1½ cups granulated sugar
- 1 cup light corn syrup
- ⅛ teaspoon kosher salt

SAUCE

- 1 cup heavy whipping cream
- 8 ounces bittersweet chocolate (I use El Rey's 70 percent bittersweet Venezuelan), chopped
- 2 tablespoons unsalted butter
- ¼ teaspoon kosher salt
- 1 tablespoon vanilla extract
- 2 tablespoons Kahlúa, rum, or bourbon (optional), for the R-rated version

- 1 cup sliced almonds for topping

To make the crust: In a medium bowl, stir together the graham cracker crumbs, powdered sugar, melted butter, and toasted almonds. Pressing hard, pack the crumb mixture evenly over the bottom of a 9 by 13-inch pan. Refrigerate until the marshmallow topping is ready.

To make the topping: Using an electric mixer fitted with the whisk attachment, beat the gelatin and ½ cup of the water in a medium bowl until thoroughly combined. Meanwhile, heat the sugar, corn syrup, the remaining ½ cup water, and salt in a medium saucepan over medium-high heat without stirring until the mixture reaches the soft-ball stage (234° to 240°F on a candy thermometer). Add the warm sugar mixture to the gelatin mixture in a slow, thin stream while beating on low speed. Increase to high speed and beat for about 5 minutes, until the mixture has thickened and cooled.

To make the sauce: In a medium saucepan, whisk the cream and chocolate over medium-low heat until the chocolate has melted. Whisk in the butter until it melts. Remove the sauce from the heat and stir in the salt, vanilla, and Kahlúa, rum, or bourbon.

Preheat the oven to 350°F. Spread the almonds on a baking sheet in a single layer and toast them in the oven for 4 to 5 minutes, until golden brown and aromatic.

To assemble the s'mores: Remove the graham cracker crust from the refrigerator and evenly cover it with the marshmallow topping. Refrigerate, uncovered, for at least 1 hour or up to 3 days. When ready to serve, brown the s'mores in the broiler before cutting them into squares or, if you're feeling dramatic, grab your kitchen torch and fire up your guests' s'mores until the marshmallow turns golden brown right in front of their eyes. (Shy types can torch the marshmallow in the privacy of their own kitchens.)

If you are using a kitchen torch, cut the s'mores into 16 squares. Using a metal spatula, transfer as many as needed to dessert plates. Hold the torch 2 to 3 inches away from the marshmallow topping and move the flame around slowly until the topping is evenly browned.

If you are using the oven, position an oven rack in the center of the oven and preheat the broiler. Broil the s'mores until the marshmallow topping turns golden brown, about 1 minute. Watch them carefully, as they can burn quickly.

Accompany with pitchers of warm chocolate sauce for guests to pour for themselves, along with bowls of toasted almonds for sprinkling over their chocolate-covered creations.

RATHER SWEET VARIATION

If you don't have time or the inclination to make the chocolate sauce, just melt as much bittersweet chocolate in the microwave as you desire, drizzle it over the torched marshmallow topping, and serve. Now, you have portable s'mores.

TIP: For extra-thick marshmallow s'mores, double the marshmallow topping in the master recipe.

Chocolate-Dipped
Peanut Butter Sandwich Bites

The idea for this cookie began when I found a carefully handwritten recipe among my mother's things. Someone must have given it to her, probably copied from a book or magazine. (It's a standard peanut butter cookie recipe.) I made a few slight changes, created a creamy peanut butter filling, spread it between two cookies, and then gave my peanut butter sandwich a half dip in melted bittersweet chocolate. Move over, Oreos—in my book, peanut butter sandwich cookies are king.

Yield: About 30 sandwich cookies

½ cup (1 stick) unsalted butter at room temperature

¾ cup smooth peanut butter

½ cup granulated sugar

½ cup firmly packed brown sugar

1 large egg

1½ cups all-purpose flour

½ teaspoon baking powder

¾ teaspoon baking soda

¼ teaspoon kosher salt

FILLING

2 cups crunchy peanut butter

½ cup (1 stick) unsalted butter at room temperature

¼ cup heavy whipping cream

½ cup powdered sugar

¼ cup firmly packed brown sugar

1 teaspoon vanilla extract

¼ teaspoon kosher salt

COATING

10 ounces bittersweet chocolate, coarsely chopped

1 cup honey-roasted peanuts, coarsely chopped (optional)

Preheat the oven to 375°F. Line baking sheets with parchment paper or silicone mats, or grease generously with butter or cooking spray.

Using an electric mixer fitted with the paddle attachment, beat the butter and peanut butter in a large bowl on medium speed until combined, then add the granulated and brown sugars and beat until fluffy, about 1 minute. Add the egg and beat on medium speed until combined. In a medium bowl, stir together the flour, baking powder, baking soda, and salt. Add the flour mixture to the peanut butter mixture and beat on medium speed just until combined. Refrigerate the dough for at least 30 minutes. (The dough can be made ahead, scooped into balls, and stored in a covered container for up to 3 days.) Use a 1½-inch scoop to drop the dough 1½ inches apart onto the prepared pan. Use the tines of a fork to press the cookie flat. Bake for 7 to 10 minutes, until the cookies are deep golden brown around the edges.

To make the filling: Using an electric mixer fitted with the paddle attachment, beat the peanut butter, butter, and heavy cream together in a medium bowl on medium-high speed until light and fluffy, about 1 minute. Add the powdered sugar, brown sugar, vanilla extract, and salt and beat on medium speed until combined.

To make the coating: Bring 2 inches of water to a simmer in a saucepan. Place the chocolate in a stainless-steel bowl and set it on top of the saucepan. Stir the chocolate until it melts completely. Pour the melted chocolate into a glass measuring cup.

Meanwhile, use a spatula to spread a generous amount of filling on the flat bottom of a cookie. Top with another cookie, ridge side up. Set a wire rack on top of a sheet of waxed or parchment paper to catch chocolate drips. Dip each cookie halfway into the melted chocolate and set it on the wire rack. Sprinkle with

the chopped peanuts and let stand for about 1 hour for the chocolate to harden. The cookies will keep for about 3 days in an airtight container or up to 2 weeks in the refrigerator. Place a round of parchment paper or waxed paper between the layers of cookies.

TIP: These cookies are best when cooked until crisp. You may be tempted to remove them from the oven when they are a light golden brown, but I recommend baking them a little longer until they are a medium golden on top and a deep golden brown around the edges. The contrast in texture between the very crisp cookie and the creamy soft filling makes for an outstanding treat.

CHAPTER THREE

❄ CHRISTMAS EVE

CHRISTMAS EVE IS the flashy twin sister to Christmas Day's quiet, turkey-and-dressing, stay-at-home sibling. On Christmas Eve, my childhood excitement grew to almost unbearable heights as I slipped on my best velvet dress and patent-leather shoes. A festive dinner of succulent beef (see Green Olive Beef Tenderloin, page 117) or lamb awaited, and then the special present, the only one we were allowed to open before Christmas Day. Family friends Betty and Peter Wells threw glittering parties with caviar and cocktails, and after I got married I looked forward to the annual Christmas Eve bash thrown by my in-laws in their gracious Houston home.

Now that I live in the heart of the Texas Hill Country, the celebrations, both private and public, at the Lyndon B. Johnson National Historical Park epitomize what's best about Christmas. There's a public tree lighting attended by many of the surviving Johnson family members, including the former first lady and her daughters, as well as a gathering of the Johnsons' extended family for fellowship and feasting during the Christmas season. I met Sue Bellows, the personal chef to Lady Bird John-

son, shortly after I moved to Fredericksburg, and we've been friends ever since. (Recently Sue's daughter, Halley, came to work for me at the bakery.) When Sue told me about the feasts she creates for the former first family over the Christmas holidays, I asked if she'd share some of her holiday favorites for this book. And lucky for us, she agreed. She also invited me into the Johnson home for a glimpse of how Christmas is celebrated there.

For Sue, the Christmas season means a constant round of meals and cooking. Throughout the holidays Sue presides over the kitchen at the LBJ Ranch in nearby Stonewall (aka the Texas White House during Lyndon Baines Johnson's term as our thirty-sixth president). The former first lady's extended family arrives in time to celebrate Mrs. Johnson's birthday on December 22, and they often stay at the ranch until New Year's. Typically, more than twenty family members populate the compound, inhabiting fourteen bedrooms throughout the main house, the guest house, and the Sunset House, all of which translates into a ten-day marathon of meals for Sue.

The days start with country breakfasts of fresh-squeezed orange juice, bacon, venison sausage, toast, eggs, and biscuits. Lunch is tortilla soup, chili, tamales, and sliced prime rib or hamburgers, and dinners often feature beef or lamb, both family favorites. Sue's stuffed LBJ Ranch Crown Roast of Lamb (facing page) always makes a holiday dinner appearance, and at least once during the season, she cooks up succulent bay shrimp and oysters, delivered fresh from the bay waters near Rockport, Texas, by a friend.

Sue fixes a Mexican feast for family members to enjoy after the ceremonial lighting of a thirty-foot Christmas tree at the Lyndon B. Johnson National Historical Park. Although not open to the public, the ranch home is part of the park, which was donated by the president and first lady more than thirty years ago. Daughters Lynda Johnson Robb and Luci Johnson and families are almost always on hand, with one family member triggering the switch that lights the tree. Meanwhile, the Texas White House has been decorated throughout with lights and fresh-cut cedar swags. Sue, who also oversees all indoor decorating, erects a ten-foot noble fir in the west room, once President Johnson's office. It's hung with family photos set in metal stars, ornaments from the former first family's White House days, including those from the U.S. Congress and Secret Service.

Sue also puts up the treasured stockings that once hung in the White House. She calls each stocking, which is made from red velvet with a personalized white satin cuff, a "work of art and a personal history of its owner." Each is decorated with a Christmas tree outfitted with beaded garlands and evenly spaced jingle bells hanging from its edges. Mrs. Johnson's is adorned with the silhouettes of both daughters and her first grandson, Lyndon, as well as a beaded depiction of the White House and the call letters of the family-owned radio station. Lynda's includes a wedding book that lists the names of those in the wedding party for her White House wedding to Charles Robb.

Holiday family dinners often take place in the formal dining room, which has a set of chairs with needlepoint cushions depicting Texas wildflowers. On her seventieth birthday, Mrs. Johnson, "an environmentalist before it was in vogue" as Sue says, founded the Lady Bird Johnson Wildflower Center in Austin, dedicated to the preservation of native plants. The wildflower center recently became a part of the University of Texas in Austin. Mrs. Johnson has always been known as a consummate hostess. "She knows how to get people together over a common meal, and she brings out incredible discussions," Sue says. "And over the years, we have had the cream of the crop as far as intellects go."

Now in her nineties and with limited mobility, Mrs. Johnson especially values Christmas with family and close friends. Christmas at the Johnson Ranch "is a wonderful example of love," Sue says. "Mrs. Johnson is enveloped in three generations of people who love her."

For me, the Christmas spirit centers on food, friends, family, and love. But during the rush and stress of the holidays, I sometimes forget. The Johnson family provides inspiration for all of us to remember what is truly important on Christmas Eve and throughout the rest of the holiday season.

LBJ Ranch Crown Roast of Lamb with Rice Stuffing and Jalapeño-Mint Sauce

Former first lady Lady Bird Johnson lives at the LBJ Ranch near Stonewall, just a few miles from Fredericksburg. She and I belong to the same church and I met the Johnson family's personal chef, Sue Bellows, at our local grocery store. (It turns out she lives in my neighborhood.) Sue has worked for the Johnson family for about fifteen years. Before that, Sue worked for two of Fredericksburg's best-known restaurants, the Peach Tree and the Hill Top Cafe, where she was working when she received a call from the former first lady: "'Sue, this is Lady Bird Johnson. I would like to know if you would come work as a cook.' I said I was under contract. She asked what days I was off. 'Fine, I'll have my dinner parties on Monday and Tuesday nights.'"

Every year, Sue prepares this recipe for the holidays. She makes Zucchini Timbales (page 104) to accompany the meat.

{ Yield: 4 to 6 servings }

2 racks of lamb (6 or 7 ribs each), trimmed and frenched (see Tip)

2 tablespoons grapeseed or olive oil, plus oil for brushing

1 small red onion, finely chopped

2 stalks celery, finely chopped

2 carrots, peeled and finely chopped

2 tart green apples, such as Granny Smith or pippin, peeled, cored, and chopped

2 tablespoons sultana (golden) raisins

2 cups cooked long-grain rice

Grated zest of 1 lemon

Juice of ½ lemon

1 cup apple cider or apple juice

2 tablespoons minced fresh flat-leaf parsley

Kosher salt and freshly ground pepper to taste

SAUCE

¾ cup minced fresh mint

¼ cup white wine vinegar

1 teaspoon kosher salt

1 tablespoon natural sugar

1½ teaspoons minced seeded jalapeño pepper

Preheat the oven to 375°F. Grease a large roasting pan with oil or cooking spray. Bend each lamb rack into a semicircle and place them together to form a crown (circle). Secure the meat with skewers and tie the bone ends together with kitchen twine. (Or, ask your butcher to do this for you.) Cover the exposed bone ends with aluminum foil. Place the lamb

continued

101

on a round of parchment paper equal to the diameter of the roast and transfer to the prepared pan.

Heat the 2 tablespoons oil in a large skillet over medium heat and cook the onion and celery until the onion is translucent, about 4 minutes. Add the carrots, apples, and raisins and continue cooking. Stir in the rice, lemon zest, lemon juice, apple cider, and parsley. Season with salt and pepper. Press the rice mixture into the center of the lamb, forming it into a gentle mound on top. Brush the meat and stuffing with oil.

Roast for 1½ to 2 hours for medium to well-done (155°F to 165°F on an instant-read thermometer). For medium-rare (145°F), check the meat after 1 hour of cooking. Using a large metal spatula, transfer the roast to a platter. Remove the foil from the bone ends and top them with frills, which can be requested from your butcher when the lamb racks are purchased.

To make the sauce: Combine the mint, vinegar, salt, sugar, and jalapeño in a glass screw-top jar and shake well. Refrigerate for 6 to 12 hours before using. If sauce seems too dense, thin it with ¼ cup water before serving.

Using a sharp knife, cut between each rib. Serve 2 to 3 chops per person, accompanied with a serving of rice stuffing. Serve the jalapeño-mint sauce alongside.

TIP: Frenching is a culinary term that means to remove the meat from the top end of a rib or chop. This prepares the bone for a decorative paper frill on the end, but also spells deprivation for anyone who likes to gnaw on the crispy bone end meat. Your butcher can french the rack for you, or you can dispense with this traditional— some would say old-fashioned—touch altogether. If you don't french, you needn't bother covering the bone tips with foil.

Zucchini Timbales

Johnson family chef Sue Bellows's recipe takes the common zucchini and elevates it to holiday-caliber fare by stuffing it with a tasty bread crumb, basil, and Parmesan mixture. If Sue cannot find small zucchini, she buys longer, thicker ones (10 inches long with a 2- to 3-inch diameter) and cuts them into 1½-inch rounds for stuffing. Either way, this dish (see photo on page 102) proves to be equally popular with kids and adults.

{ **Yield: 4 to 6 servings** }

10 small zucchini, 5 to 6 inches long and
   about 1 inch in diameter

¼ cup fresh basil

1 clove garlic, peeled

½ cup freshly grated Parmesan cheese

1 large egg

¼ cup fresh or dried bread crumbs

½ teaspoon kosher salt

Preheat the oven to 350°F. Grease a large baking dish with butter or cooking spray. Slice the zucchini in half lengthwise and place them in a steamer basket in a large saucepan filled with 2 inches of simmering water. Cover and steam the zucchini until softened but not mushy, 3 to 4 minutes, or a little longer if you've used thicker zucchini. Place the steamed zucchini, cut side down, on a double layer of paper towels to drain until cool to the touch. Using a melon baller or teaspoon, scoop out and reserve the centers, leaving the outer skin and about ¼ inch of the inner flesh. (You will have about 2 cups reserved flesh.) Set aside the zucchini shells.

Combine the reserved zucchini flesh, basil, garlic, Parmesan, egg, bread crumbs, and salt in a blender or food processor. Pulse until just mixed, not puréed. Arrange the zucchini shells, skin side down, in the prepared baking dish. Using a spoon or a pastry bag, fill each shell with the filling mixture. The filling should be rounded on top but not brimming out of the shells. Bake for about 25 minutes, until golden brown on top. Serve immediately.

Ensalada de Noche Buena (Christmas Eve Salad)

Fonda San Miguel is one of my favorite Austin restaurants. More than thirty years ago, owners Miguel Ravago and Tom Gilliland bucked the Tex-Mex tide, championing authentic Mexican cuisine long before it became trendy. The hacienda-style restaurant, packed with fine art Tom has brought back from Mexico, has a romantic ambiance that's hard to resist.

The owners gave me permission to include this wonderful salad adapted from their cookbook Fonda San Miguel: Thirty Years of Food and Art. *Miguel says his grandmother used to make this salad for the holidays with her own homegrown citrus and pomegranates. For a smaller crowd, cut the recipe in half.*

{ Yield: 8 to 10 servings }

4 oranges, peeled and segmented (see Tip)

4 Red Delicious apples, peeled, cored, and diced

1 jicama, peeled and cut into matchsticks

6 beets, cooked, peeled, and diced (optional)

1 cup fresh pineapple cubes

2 bananas, sliced

1 cup unsalted roasted peanuts

¼ cup sugar

¼ cup rice vinegar

2 tablespoons olive oil

¾ cup club soda

DRESSING

Seeds of 1 pomegranate (reserve some seeds for garnish)

½ cup sour cream

¼ cup sugar

½ cup apple juice

1 head iceberg lettuce, cored and thinly sliced

Combine the oranges, apples, jicama, beets, pineapple, bananas, peanuts, sugar, vinegar, olive oil, and club soda in a large ceramic or plastic bowl. Toss to blend. Cover and refrigerate for at least 2 hours or up to 12 hours.

To make the dressing: While the salad is chilling, make the pomegranate dressing. Combine the pomegranate seeds, sour cream, sugar, and apple juice in a blender and purée.

Drain the salad in a colander. Transfer to a salad bowl and toss with the pomegranate dressing. Serve on a bed of the iceberg lettuce and garnish with the reserved pomegranate seeds.

👑 **TIP:** This is a lovely pink-tinged salad. If you wish to avoid the pink hue, do not use the optional beets and do not process the pomegranate seeds in the dressing,

continued

but sprinkle them over the salad just before dressing it.

TIP: To peel and segment an orange, use a sharp knife to cut the top and bottom off the orange. Stand the orange on one end and cut down along the sides to remove the skin and white pith. Holding the orange in your palm, carefully cut between the membranes to remove each segment.

Oysters Rockefeller Soup

Chef Steve Howard made oysters Rockefeller soup at a Christmas Eve dinner party we catered together, and it bowled me over. It reminded me of eating oysters Rockefeller in Houston as a little girl, when it seemed that every high-end restaurant in town offered the elegant dish served on the half shell. It made me feel so sophisticated and grown up. Little did I know the dish had some pretty fancy roots. Oysters Rockefeller originated at Antoine's, one of New Orleans's oldest and most famous restaurants. According to the restaurant's website, "The sauce of oysters Rockefeller was so rich and buttery, they felt it should be named after the nation's richest baron of the day, John D. Rockefeller." Although the original recipe has remained a closely guarded secret for more than one hundred years, the dish was widely admired and imitations began popping up on other restaurants' menus. Today, the best-known renditions of oysters Rockefeller include spinach as well as a rich butter, herb, and bread crumb topping infused with an anise-flavored liqueur such as Herbsaint or Pernod. Oddly enough, the original was reportedly made with watercress, not spinach. I haven't a clue as to when the idea emerged to use the elements of oysters Rockefeller to make a soup, but it has been around long enough to spawn many variations on the theme. Most, including Steve's, use spinach.

{ **Yield: 6 servings** }

5 tablespoons unsalted butter

2 cups diced onions

1 tablespoon minced garlic

½ cup all-purpose flour

2 cups bottled clam juice

½ cup dry white wine

2½ cups chopped fresh spinach

¾ cup Herbsaint or Pernod liqueur

½ cup heavy whipping cream

½ cup crumbled blue cheese

½ teaspoon kosher salt

½ teaspoon ground white pepper

Dash of Tabasco sauce

Dash of Worcestershire sauce

1 pint fresh oysters with oyster liquor

Melt 4 tablespoons of the butter in a large stockpot over medium heat. Add the onions and sauté until translucent, 4 to 6 minutes. Add the garlic, reduce the heat to medium-low, and sauté for 1 minute more, making sure the garlic does not burn. Whisk in the flour and cook for 2 to 3 minutes, whisking steadily. Whisk in the clam juice and reduce the heat to medium-low. Cook until the mixture thickens, stirring frequently, about 5 minutes. Add the wine and cook for 5 more minutes, stirring occasionally. Remove from the heat while you prepare the spinach mixture.

In a large skillet, melt the remaining 1 tablespoon butter over medium heat. Add the spinach and sauté until it cooks down, 2 or 3 minutes. Stir in ¼ cup of the Herbsaint or Pernod and cook about 3 minutes more. Stir the spinach mixture into the onion and clam juice mixture. Add the cream, blue cheese, and the remaining ½ cup liqueur. Stir until the mixture is hot but not boiling. Add the salt, pepper, Tabasco, and Worcestershire. Taste and adjust the seasoning. Add the oysters, let them cook a few minutes, then serve immediately.

TIP: Herbsaint liqueur is an anise-flavored spirit made in New Orleans and difficult to find outside of the South. Pernod, available at most liquor stores, is a good substitute.

Blue Corn Blinis with Crab and Avocado Crema

David Garrido, a great friend and a wonderful chef, used to serve blue corn blinis with caviar and crème fraîche during the holidays. His love for caviar and his encyclopedic knowledge of the world's most famous luxury food meant that he always had access to the best available. I recently called David to ask him for the blini recipe. He shared the ingredients with me, but provided no measurements. "It's easy, just like pancake batter," he said. "You'll figure it out." I did, and while I was at it, I gave it a Texas twist—using lump crabmeat, a creamy avocado sauce, and pico de gallo, which turned out to be a great combination with the coarse-textured blue corn pancakes.

This recipe looks like a lot of work, but you can ease the load by using store-bought mayonnaise, and by making the blini batter, pico de gallo, and avocado crema in advance and refrigerating each in covered containers for up to one day. If refrigerated, let the blini batter stand at room temperature for about an hour before cooking.

I like to serve blinis crisp and warm from the griddle as appetizers. You can assemble them for guests, or you can set out the fixings and let guests pile on the ingredients themselves.

{ Yield: About 28 appetizer servings }

1 teaspoon active dry yeast

2 tablespoons warm (110° to 115°F) water

½ cup blue cornmeal flour

7 tablespoons all-purpose flour

¼ teaspoon kosher salt

½ cup milk

3 tablespoons unsalted butter, melted

AVOCADO CREMA

1 ripe avocado, peeled and pitted

¼ cup mayonnaise (page 55) or store-bought mayo

¼ cup plain yogurt

1½ teaspoons freshly squeezed lemon juice

2 dashes Tabasco sauce

¼ teaspoon kosher salt, or to taste

8 ounces fresh lump crabmeat, picked over for shell

1 tablespoon freshly squeezed lime juice

Pico de Gallo (page 93)

Preheat a griddle to 350°F or set a griddle or large, heavy skillet over medium-high heat. Stir the yeast into the water in a small bowl. Let stand until foamy, about 5 minutes. In a medium bowl, stir together the flours and salt. Add the milk, yeast mixture, and butter, whisking to combine after each addition. Let the mixture sit at room temperature for about 10 minutes. Coat the preheated griddle or skillet with cooking spray. Use 1 tablespoon

continued

of batter per blini and cook for 2 to 3 minutes on each side, until crisp around the edges and golden brown.

To make the avocado crema: Pulse the avocado in a food processor until smooth. Add the mayonnaise, yogurt, lemon juice, Tabasco, and salt and process until smooth. Spoon into a squeeze bottle and refrigerate until ready to use. (The crema can be made 1 day in advance.)

To assemble the blinis: In a small bowl, break the crabmeat into small chunks and stir in the lime juice to coat. Squeeze about ¼ teaspoon of crema on each blini and top with about 1 teaspoon of the crabmeat mixture. Spoon about 1 teaspoon of pico de gallo on top of the crabmeat and top it off with an artful squiggle of crema. Serve immediately.

♛ **TIP:** Stone-ground blue cornmeal flour is available at Whole Foods and many other natural foods stores, often in the bulk foods section.

♛ **TIP:** If you don't have a squeeze bottle on hand to dispense the crema, use a small sandwich-sized plastic bag. Fill it no more than two-thirds full and snip a tiny bit off the bag's corner with sharp scissors. Squeeze lightly to push the desired amount of crema onto the blinis.

Mascarpone Grits Cakes

Grits, made from ground corn, are a Southern staple, and I grew up eating them often for breakfast with a bit of milk, butter, and sugar. Here, I've taken a traditional fried grits recipe and added a taste of mascarpone cheese (a very rich Italian-style cream cheese) to give the grits a luxurious, creamy quality that's perfect as a holiday dinner side dish. Then I cut the grits into rounds, squares, or whatever shape fits the occasion, and I fry them up until they are golden crisp on the outside and still creamy on the inside.

{ **Yield: About 22 cakes** }

2½ cups milk

1 cup half-and-half

½ cup (1 stick) unsalted butter

1½ teaspoons kosher salt

1¼ cups quick grits

1 cup freshly grated Parmesan cheese

⅔ cup (5 ounces) mascarpone cheese

½ teaspoon freshly ground pepper

Grease a 9 by 13-inch baking pan with butter or cooking spray. In a large saucepan, bring the milk, half-and-half, butter, and salt to a boil. Reduce the heat to medium and gradually whisk in grits. Whisk constantly until cooked and thickened. (Follow package directions for the cooking time, which will depend on the type of grits you use.) Whisk in the Parmesan, mascarpone, and pepper until incorporated.

Pour the grits in the prepared pan and refrigerate until set, about 1 hour. Use a biscuit cutter (or holiday cookie cutter of your choice) to cut the grits into shapes about 2 inches in

diameter. Or, cut the grits into squares or triangles to avoid scraps. The cakes can be made ahead until this point, wrapped and refrigerated for up to 2 days, then finished in a skillet when ready to serve. Or, keep the grits warm and covered in the baking pan and panfry them just before serving.

Grease a large skillet with cooking spray or a light film of olive oil and place it over medium heat. When the skillet is hot, cook the cakes in batches, leaving a little space between each one in the pan. Fry the cakes for 2 to 3 minutes per side, or until browned and crisp. Serve immediately.

RATHER SWEET VARIATION

Add any minced fresh herb or flavoring of your choice, such as green onion, garlic, parsley, rosemary, or thyme. For a less rich version, substitute 3½ cups 2 percent milk or low-fat milk for the milk and half-and-half.

Holiday Martinis

"What a great base for a holiday martini," I thought as I contemplated a bottle of prickly pear syrup ordered from the Internet. I headed over to see friends Dan and Kim Robertson, hoping they'd help me test the idea. Dan Robertson is my orthopedic surgeon—he was a doctor for the San Diego Chargers before he and Kim moved to Fredericksburg—and his wife, Kim, is one of my dearest friends here. We spent the evening mixing various boozy concoctions using the deep red-pink syrup, made from the fruit of the Southwest's ubiquitous prickly pear cactus. As the night wore on, and we continued to test (and taste) each one, our cocktail names became increasingly clever and hilarious. (Or, at least we thought so.) Dan dubbed the tequila-spiked martini the Pink Slip—one drink too many, and you won't show up for work the next day. Another became the Pink Cadillac, because we were certain we had created the Cadillac of all martinis. After that, the names flowed as easily as the rum, vodka, and tequila: Prickly in Pink, Pink Panther, Pink Predator, and finally, Deadly in Pink. In the end, I left the Robertson home having coined yet another name: "Dan, the Martini Man." Below are the best two drinks we developed that night.

Prickly in Pink Martini

{ Yield: 1 serving }

2 ounces vodka

½ ounce Triple Sec

½ ounce prickly pear syrup

1 teaspoon freshly squeezed lime juice

Cracked ice for shaking

Shake the vodka, Triple Sec, syrup, and lime juice in a cocktail shaker filled with cracked ice. Strain into a martini glass and serve immediately.

Texas Sunset

{ Yield: 1 serving }

½ ounce citrus-flavored rum (we used Bacardi Limón Rum)

2 ounces vodka

½ ounce prickly pear syrup

Squeeze of lime

Cracked ice for shaking

Shake the rum, vodka, syrup, and lime juice in a cocktail shaker filled with cracked ice. Strain into a martini glass and serve immediately.

TIP: The night of our martini fest, Kim had a freezer full of frozen green grapes. (Her kids love to snack on them.) We dropped grapes in our martinis, and they kept the drinks

continued

ice cold without watering them down. Next, we stuck toothpicks in a few unfrozen grapes and tucked them in the freezer. We slipped these frozen grapes in our martinis, and they looked like traditional martini olives. Eating a martini-infused grape is a delicious treat.

♛ **TIP:** You can order Cheri's Desert Harvest Prickly Pear Syrup by calling 800-743-1141 or visiting www.cherisdesertharvest.com.

Martha's Best-Ever Rolls

The moment I tasted Martha's mother's rolls, soft and pillowy, slightly sweet, and redolent of yeast, I knew I needed the recipe. Now retired and living in Fredericksburg, Martha Craig spent many years working with her husband, Bill, on their large cattle ranch in eastern Colorado.

"I did the branding and the cooking. I'd make the rolls and stick them up on the kitchen counter to rise. Then I'd run out to do a few more brands." Martha learned to make rolls with her mother, an elegant Kentucky-bred woman. The family lived in San Antonio and had a cook, but Martha's mother always made the rolls, the cakes, and the ham.

When Martha moved with her husband to their eastern Colorado ranch, her mother was "horrified," but when it came to making rolls, mother and daughter saw eye to eye. Neither of them measured ingredients; they added flour or milk and stirred the dough until it felt right. Before she made the recipe in my kitchen, Martha couldn't tell me exactly how much flour she used. Martha insists there's a lot of latitude when making the rolls. "You can't hurt it [the dough] if you add a little more flour or a little more milk."

These are not last-minute rolls. They rise twice, and must be refrigerated overnight in between. I think they are worth every minute of preparation time.

{ Yield: About 32 rolls }

FIRST-STAGE DOUGH

1¼ cups warm water (110°F to 115°F)

1 package active dry yeast

Pinch of sugar, plus 1 cup

Pinch of all-purpose flour, plus 3¾ cups

3¼ cups milk

1 cup canola oil

SECOND-STAGE DOUGH

1 tablespoon kosher salt

1 tablespoon baking powder

¼ teaspoon baking soda

7 to 8 cups plus ¼ cup all-purpose flour

First-Stage Dough, above

Butter for serving

To make the first-stage dough: In a small bowl, stir together the water, yeast, pinch of sugar, and pinch of flour. (The sugar and flour feed the yeast, activating it and making it bubble more quickly and fiercely.) Let the mixture sit until foamy, 5 to 10 minutes.

Heat the milk in a large saucepan over medium-high heat until it begins to steam. (Do not boil it.) Pour the hot milk into a large heatproof bowl and stir in the oil, the 1 cup sugar, and ¼ cup of the flour. Stir constantly until the milk mixture cools to between 110° to 115°F on a candy thermometer.

Add the yeast to the milk mixture. Gradually whisk in the remaining 3½ cups flour about ½ cup at a time. The batter should be thin, similar to the consistency of pancake batter.

Cover the bowl with plastic wrap, parchment paper, or a clean tea towel, and let stand in a warm place for about 1 hour, until the dough doubles in bulk.

To make the second-stage dough: Stir together the salt, baking powder, baking soda, and 1 cup of the flour in a small bowl. Stir this mixture into the first-stage dough until all ingredients are combined. Continue stirring in the flour, ½ cup at a time, until the dough starts to lose its stickiness and begins to pull away from the sides of the pan as you stir. (I use my hands so I can feel when the dough is the right consistency.) Once the dough is at that stage, cover the top and sides with about ¼ cup flour, gently pulling the dough away from the sides of the bowl with a spoon and letting some of the flour slip down the sides. Cover the bowl with plastic wrap and refrigerate overnight. At this point, the dough will keep for up to 3 days.

Preheat the oven to 400°F. Evenly coat a 9-inch cake pan with cooking spray or butter. Use a sharp knife to cut off hunks of dough about the size of a small lemon. Set each dough ball in the cake pan (about 8 should fit, with 6 around the edges and 2 in the middle). The rolls should be barely touching, so they have room to expand. Set them in a warm spot until light and puffy, similar in texture to a soft marshmallow. (Depending on the warmth of your kitchen, this could take from 30 minutes to more than 1 hour.) Bake for 15 to 20 minutes, until the rolls are golden brown on top. Serve immediately with butter.

RATHER SWEET VARIATION

Once the dough has been refrigerated overnight, you have the perfect base for Bite-Sized Sticky Buns (page 79).

Green Olive Beef Tenderloin

My mother often made this on Christmas Eve and I always loved it, but she never gave me the recipe. Over the years, I've dreamed about eating it again and wished she'd left me instructions. When I started writing this book, I knew I had to include it, so I figured I would have to re-create it from memory. The olives were all my mind could conjure up, plus a little salt, pepper, and olive oil, so that's where I started. The olive-topped tenderloin emerged from the oven. I cut into it and took a cautious bite. It was perfect. In a single Proustian moment, I saw my mother's glittering holiday parties unfurling in front of me and remembered how much she loved to entertain.

{ Yield: 6 to 8 servings }

3 pounds beef tenderloin, trimmed

¼ cup olive oil

1 tablespoon kosher salt

2 teaspoons freshly ground pepper

2 cups large pimiento-stuffed green olives, halved

¼ to ½ cup olive juice from the green olives

Coat the tenderloin with olive oil and sprinkle with the salt and pepper. Let stand at room temperature for 1 hour.

Preheat the oven to 500°F. Sear the tenderloin in an extra-large sauté pan for about 1 minute on each side, or until it is nicely browned. Place the tenderloin in a roasting pan. Spread the olives across the top of the meat and pour the olive juice evenly over everything. Roast for 9 minutes (3 minutes per pound), then turn off the oven and leave the roast undisturbed for 45 minutes (for medium-rare). Do not open the oven door during this time. Remove from the oven and loosely tent with aluminum foil. Let rest for 15 to 20 minutes. Carve and serve.

TIP: Let the roast stay in the oven for 1 hour if you prefer your meat medium or medium-well.

TIP: It seems hard to imagine that you'll have much in the way of leftovers, but if you do, there's nothing better than a tenderloin sandwich served on a soft roll. Try it on a leftover Martha's Best-Ever Rolls (page 114) with a touch of horseradish or a slathering of horseradish sauce (below).

RATHER SWEET VARIATION

Although this roast is wonderful as is, I often serve it with a simple homemade horseradish sauce: In a medium bowl, combine 1 cup mayonnaise, ½ cup sour cream, ¼ cup prepared horseradish (or more to taste), and 1 tablespoon freshly squeezed lemon juice. Pass the sauce in a serving dish as an accompaniment to the tenderloin.

Sticky Toffee Pudding with Brandy Butterscotch Sauce

I often stop by Cappy's Restaurant after teaching a class at San Antonio's Central Market. I love the restaurant and its owners, Cappy and Suzy Lawton. They were pioneers in the resurgence of San Antonio's Alamo Heights neighborhood, opening the restaurant in 1977, when few saw the run-down neighborhood's potential. Today, the area is bursting with successful restaurants and businesses. Sticky toffee pudding is a Christmastime tradition in England. Cappy's version, a popular selection on his menu all year long, is relatively easy to make. The key to success is a 9-inch glass pie plate. Make sure you have one before you start. If you don't, they are often available for a reasonable price at larger grocery stores.

{ Yield: 6 to 8 servings }

1 cup sugar

1 large egg

1 tablespoon smooth apricot jam

1 cup all-purpose flour

1 teaspoon baking soda

½ teaspoon kosher salt

1 cup milk

1 tablespoon unsalted butter

1 teaspoon distilled white vinegar

SAUCE

¾ cup (1½ sticks) unsalted butter

1 cup heavy whipping cream

1 cup sugar

½ cup hot water

1 tablespoon brandy

Vanilla bean ice cream for serving

Preheat the oven to 450°F. Grease a 9-inch glass pie plate with butter or cooking spray. Using an electric mixer fitted with the paddle attachment, beat the sugar, egg, and jam on high speed for 15 minutes. (Yes, 15 minutes. Do not try to cheat to save time. I tried it, and the recipe didn't work.) In a medium bowl, stir together the flour, baking soda, and salt to blend. Add the milk and flour mixture alternately to the egg mixture in 3 increments. After each addition, beat on low speed until combined. Melt the butter in a small saucepan over medium heat and stir in the vinegar. Add the butter mixture to the flour mixture and beat on medium-low speed until combined.

Pour the batter into the prepared pie plate. Cover with aluminum foil that has been greased with butter or cooking spray and bake for 35 to 45 minutes, until the pudding is a rich, brown color. If it is still pale in the center, cook a little longer. Just before the pudding is done, make the sauce.

To make the sauce: Melt the butter with the cream, sugar, hot water, and brandy over medium heat, stirring until blended and hot. Pour half the sauce over the pudding immediately after you remove it from the oven. As soon as the sauce is absorbed, pour the remaining sauce over the pudding. (The pudding can be made up to 3 days ahead, stored tightly covered in the refrigerator and reheated on high in the microwave for about 1 minute, until heated through.) Cut into wedges and serve hot, with vanilla bean ice cream.

Apple Dumplings

When cinnamon-sugar–infused apples are wrapped in flaky piecrust dough and baked half-submerged in cinnamon-sugar syrup, the result is irresistible. Marie Comstock, the mother of a good friend of mine, gave me this recipe. She made it for me once, and I had to have it. She calls it "a good diversion from pie" and can't remember exactly where it came from, but figures she copied it out of one of her sixties-era cookbooks. She uses her favorite piecrust recipe made with vegetable oil, not shortening or butter, a heart-healthier way to go. "My children grew up on these," Marie says. Lucky them. An extra bonus: As these dumplings bake, the kitchen fills with the sweet scent of cinnamon, enveloping you and your guests in a cozy holiday feeling. For larger parties, the recipe can be doubled.

{ **Yield: 6 servings** }

CRUST

3½ cups all-purpose flour

½ teaspoon kosher salt

1 cup canola oil

½ cup water

SYRUP

1 teaspoon ground cinnamon

2 cups sugar

2 cups water

6 tablespoons unsalted butter

2 cups sugar

2 tablespoons ground cinnamon

6 small or medium Granny Smith apples

3 teaspoons unsalted butter

To make the crust: Preheat the oven to 400°F. Grease a 9 by 13-inch square baking pan with butter or cooking spray. Combine the flour and salt in a medium bowl. Using your hands, mix the oil into the flour mixture, then add the water and mix just until the dough is smooth. Gently form the dough into a disk.

To make the syrup: Stir the cinnamon and sugar together in a medium saucepan. Stir in the water and bring to a boil over high heat. Reduce the heat to a simmer and cook for 3 to 4 minutes, until the syrup is slightly thickened. Stir in the butter until melted. Remove the syrup from the heat.

To assemble the dumplings: Break the dough into 6 equal pieces. On a work surface, use a rolling pin to separately roll each piece of dough between 2 sheets of waxed paper. The dough should be between ⅛ to ¼ inch thick and big enough to cover one apple with about ½ inch to spare around the edges. Gently peel off the top layer of waxed paper to loosen it (leaving it in place), then invert the dough. Gently peel the waxed paper from the other side. Loosening the dough from the waxed paper makes it easier to wrap the apples later. Repeat until you have 6 pieces of rolled-out pie dough.

Stir together the sugar and cinnamon in a small bowl. Peel and core the apples. Set each apple in the middle of a rolled-out piece of dough. Remember to remove the top piece of waxed paper. Fill the center of the apple three-fourths full of cinnamon-sugar and top it with ½ teaspoon butter. Fold the opposite sides of the dough over the top of the apple so they overlap. Press the dough seams together. Repeat with the two remaining sides, making sure to firmly press the seams together. Fill the remaining apples with the cinnamon-sugar and butter and wrap them in the dough as described above.

Place the wrapped apples seam side up without touching in the prepared pan. Pour the cinnamon-sugar syrup into the bottom of the pan, not over the tops of the apples. Bake for 45 minutes to 1 hour, until the crust is golden brown. Serve warm, with the cinnamon-sugar syrup poured over the apples.

TIP: Try apple dumplings à la mode by serving them in bowls topped with your favorite flavor of ice cream. I recommend the highest-quality vanilla bean ice cream you can find. Looking for something more exotic? Try ginger ice cream.

Christmas Coconut Cake

This Christmas cake will make your friends gasp: three white cake layers covered with a light snowfall of flaked coconut. This recipe came from my Great-Aunt Molly, who always used fresh coconut milk in her cake. If I'm feeling unusually energetic, I do the same (see Tip). Otherwise, I substitute coconut cream, which is a lot easier to manage.

My cousin Vera Mitchell Garlough used to make this cake with her mother and sister. Vera wrote: "Mama used the standard boiled frosting from her Searchlight Cookbook, 1931 printing. The method called for boiling sugar and water until it made a thread when dripped from a spoon, then adding the very hot syrup very slowly to stiffly beaten egg whites, beating all the time. Then, we did not have the luxury of an electric mixer in our home so sister Barbara and I, while young girls, learned to make this frosting as a team. She poured while I beat, then she beat while I poured—using an old wire whisk. Somehow, it became stiff and always turned out right and we never scalded ourselves with the hot syrup. In later years, when she bought a double boiler, Mama used this standard recipe, which I use today."

{ Yield: 8 to 10 servings }

1 cup (2 sticks) unsalted butter at room temperature

2 cups sugar

3 cups all-purpose flour

4 teaspoons baking powder

½ teaspoon kosher salt

¼ cup whole milk

½ cup unsweetened coconut milk (available canned in the Asian section of most grocery stores, or see Tip)

¼ cup coconut cream (Coco Lopez)

1 teaspoon vanilla extract

8 large egg whites at room temperature

WHIPPED CREAM FILLING

1 cup cold heavy whipping cream

2 tablespoons coconut cream (Coco Lopez)

½ cup grated fresh coconut (optional, see Tip)

FROSTING

2 large egg whites

1½ cups sugar

⅓ cup cold water

¼ teaspoon cream of tartar

¼ teaspoon kosher salt

½ cup mini marshmallows

1 teaspoon vanilla extract

3 to 4 cups unsweetened flaked coconut for decorating

Place an oven rack in the bottom third of the oven and another in the top third of the oven. Preheat the oven to 350°F. Butter three 9-inch cake pans, then line each with a parchment paper round. Butter the paper and dust the pans with flour; knock out the excess.

continued

Using an electric mixer fitted with the paddle attachment, cream the butter and sugar on medium-high speed until light and fluffy, about 3 minutes. Use a rubber spatula to scrape down the sides of the bowl. In a medium bowl, stir together the flour, baking powder, and salt to blend. In a small bowl, stir together the milk, coconut milk, and coconut cream until smooth. Add the flour mixture in 3 increments, alternating with the milk mixture in 2 increments, starting and ending with the flour mixture. After each addition, mix at low speed just to combine the ingredients. Stir in the vanilla.

Using an electric mixer fitted with the whisk attachment, beat the egg whites on high speed until stiff peaks form. Gently fold the egg whites into the batter until evenly blended. Divide the cake batter evenly among the prepared cake pans. Set two layers on the top rack and the third on the lower rack. Stagger the cake layers on the oven racks so that

no layer is directly over another. Bake for 35 minutes, or until a toothpick inserted in the middle of the cakes comes out clean. Monitor the layers carefully for doneness; each one may be done at a different time. Remove from the oven and let cool in the pans for 10 minutes, then unmold onto wire racks to cool completely.

To make the whipped cream filling: Using an electric mixer fitted with the whisk attachment, beat the cream on high speed until soft peaks form. Beat in the coconut cream and the fresh coconut, if using.

To make the frosting: Whisk the egg whites, sugar, water, cream of tartar, and salt in a large stainless-steel bowl until thoroughly combined. Place the bowl over a saucepan filled with 2 inches of barely simmering water. Using a hand beater or handheld electric mixer, continue beating the egg white mixture for 4 minutes. Add the mini marshmallows in

2 increments while continuing to beat. Wait until the first batch of marshmallows has melted before adding the second. Continue beating for 2 to 3 minutes more, until stiff peaks form. Remove from the heat, stir in the vanilla, and continue beating until the frosting is thick enough to spread.

To assemble the cake: Stack one cake layer on a serving plate and spread the top with half of the whipped cream filling. Repeat with a second layer. Stack the final cake layer on top of the first two and cover the cake's top and sides with the frosting. Sprinkle the coconut on the top and sides of the cake.

Cover the cake loosely with plastic wrap and store for 1 day at room temperature or up to 3 days in the refrigerator. Bring to room temperature before serving.

TIP: It's challenging to press coconut into the sides of the cake. When pressing the coconut in, the icing invariably sticks to my fingers and mars the frosting's finish. I've discovered that throwing small handfuls of coconut toward the side of the cake makes it adhere quite well—a messy but effective technique for creating a gorgeous-looking cake.

TIP: For those who want to follow Aunt Molly's original recipe, here are her directions for extracting coconut meat and liquid from a fresh coconut: "First buy a fresh coconut. To select the best one, shake it to listen for a lot of milk inside. Prepare the coconut by first making a hole or two in one end with a hammer and ice pick. Stand the coconut up over a small bowl or glass measuring cup to catch the milk as it drains out. Next, crack the hard outer shell with a hammer, then pry off the pieces. The inner white coconut meat can then be grated [with a handheld microplane grater]. Refrigerate both the milk and grated coconut until ready to use."

Hot Mocha Cakes

A sophisticated adults-only dessert, these cakes are beyond chocolatey. I use almost a pound of bittersweet chocolate to create small, intensely chocolate cakes with soft, gooey centers. Surprisingly simple to make, the cakes are a godsend for busy cooks, because they can be assembled in advance, refrigerated, and baked just before serving.

Bittersweet chocolate with at least 70 percent cacao elevates this dessert to the pinnacle of its chocolate potential. I use El Rey 70 percent bittersweet. I'm a big fan of this strong, fruity chocolate imported from Venezuela. Lucky for us, Rand Turner, president of Chocolate El Rey, lives in Fredericksburg. If he's in town, you'll find Rand sitting at his regular table at the Rather Sweet Bakery & Café between 8 and 9 A.M. Monday through Friday, drinking coffee, chatting, and wisecracking his way through the hour with his buddies Bob and Bruce. Rand feels so at home here that he brings his personal chocolate stash to sweeten his coffee, and lately, he's taken to storing a carton of Borden's milk in our refrigerator. He says it reminds him of his childhood. The bakery goes through about twenty-two pounds of El Rey chocolate a week, and during busy times we'll finish off more than forty pounds. El Rey chocolate is not cheap, but it is among the best available. Look for it at upscale grocery stores or on the company website at www. chocolates-elrey.com.

{ Yield: 6 servings }

14 ounces 70 percent bittersweet chocolate, coarsely chopped

4 tablespoons unsalted butter at room temperature

½ cup sugar

Pinch of kosher salt

3 large eggs

2 large egg yolks

⅓ cup all-purpose flour

2 teaspoons powdered espresso stirred into 1 teaspoon boiling water

2 tablespoons Kahlúa liqueur

1 teaspoon vanilla extract

Vanilla bean ice cream or crème fraîche or lightly sweetened whipped heavy cream for serving

Preheat the oven to 400°F. Generously grease six ¾-cup ovenproof ramekins or custard cups with butter or cooking spray. If you plan to bake the cakes immediately after mixing the batter, place a baking sheet in the oven for preheating.

In a large bowl set over a saucepan filled with 2 inches of simmering water, melt the chocolate. Stir until the chocolate is smooth, and set it aside to cool. Using an electric mixer fitted with the paddle attachment, cream the butter and sugar on medium speed until light and fluffy, about 2 minutes. Add the salt, eggs, and egg yolks and beat on medium speed until well mixed. (The batter will look a bit curdled.) Add the melted chocolate and beat until blended. Add the flour and beat until the batter smooths out. Add the espresso, Kahlúa, and vanilla and beat to blend. Evenly spoon the batter into the prepared ramekins or cups. (The cakes can be made in advance up to this point. Cover the ramekins or cups with plastic wrap and refrigerate for up to 2 days.)

Place the ramekins or cups on the heated baking sheet in the oven. Bake for 10 to 14 minutes, until the cakes are no longer shiny around the edges and are still loose in the middle. The cakes may take 1 or 2 minutes more if they've been refrigerated before baking. Remove from the oven and the baking pan and let cool for about 3 minutes. Unmold each cake onto a dessert plate and top with a scoop of ice cream or a dollop of crème fraîche or lightly sweetened whipped cream. Serve immediately.

TIP: These are so rich you may wish to make smaller cakes. I've used 2-inch ramekins with great success. Watch them carefully though, as they will take less time to bake than the larger versions.

Warm Pear Ginger Upside-Down Cake with Amaretto Whipped Cream

Before you start this recipe, make sure you have the proper pan: You'll need a 9- or 10-inch cake pan with sides that are at least 2 inches tall. (Most standard 9-inch cake pans have 1-inch sides, which will leave you with overflowing batter.) If you strike out in the cake pan department, an ovenproof skillet with similar dimensions will work. This cake is so fabulous, I would strongly consider buying a 9 by 2-inch cake pan especially for this recipe. It's surprisingly easy to make, and as a finale for a holiday dinner party it is as dramatic as it is delectable. Best warm from the oven, it will still taste good at room temperature. It retains its peak flavor and texture throughout the day it's made.

{ Yield: 6 to 8 servings }

TOPPING

- ½ cup (1 stick) salted butter
- ½ cup firmly packed dark brown sugar
- 2 to 3 ripe but firm pears, such as Anjou or Bartlett
- 2 tablespoons finely chopped candied ginger

CAKE

- ½ cup (1 stick) unsalted butter at room temperature
- 1 cup granulated sugar
- 2 large eggs
- 1⅓ cups all-purpose flour
- 1½ teaspoons baking powder
- ¼ teaspoon kosher salt
- ½ cup milk
- 1½ teaspoons vanilla extract
- 2 tablespoons finely chopped candied ginger

WHIPPED CREAM

- 1 cup cold heavy whipping cream
- ¼ cup powdered sugar
- 1 tablespoon Amaretto liqueur

To make the topping: Preheat the oven to 350°F. Put the butter and brown sugar in the cake pan and place it in the oven until melted and bubbly, about 10 minutes. Core the pears (no need to peel them) and cut them into ¼-inch-thick slices. Remove the pan from the oven, stir to combine the butter and sugar, and arrange the pears on top of the mixture in a circular pattern. Don't worry if you end up with a second layer of pears. Sprinkle the candied ginger evenly over the pears.

To make the cake: Using an electric mixer fitted with the paddle attachment, cream the butter and sugar together on medium-high speed until light and fluffy, about 3 minutes.

Add the eggs and beat for another 30 seconds. Stir together the flour, baking powder, and salt in a separate bowl. To the butter mixture, add the flour mixture in 3 increments alternating with the milk in 2 increments, starting and ending with the flour, beating on low speed between each addition. Stir in the vanilla and candied ginger. Pour the batter evenly over the pears. Bake for about 45 minutes if using a 10-inch pan and about 55 minutes for a 9-incher. The cake is done when a toothpick inserted in the center comes out clean. Remove from the oven and immediately invert onto a large cake plate. Let cool for about 15 minutes. Meanwhile, make the whipped cream.

To make the whipped cream: Using an electric mixer fitted with the whisk attachment, beat the cream on high speed until soft peaks form. Beat in the powdered sugar and Amaretto.

Serve the cake, slightly warm, with the whipped cream alongside.

RATHER SWEET VARIATION

Skip the whipped cream and serve this cake with a high-quality vanilla ice cream. Warm cake, cold ice cream melting on caramelized pears . . . yum.

Mini Bourbon-Macadamia Nut Pies

I cannot seem to survive the holidays without making (and eating) some kind of nut pie. Recently, I developed a hankering for something other than the tried-and-true pecan version, so I switched to macadamias and made the pies small enough for individual servings. I always make a large batch, because these small pies can be wrapped and frozen for up to 1 month. That way, there's always a sweet dessert on hand when holiday guests arrive unexpectedly.

{ Yield: 2 dozen pies }

2½ cups all-purpose flour

½ teaspoon kosher salt

⅔ cup granulated sugar

⅔ cup (1⅓ sticks) cold unsalted butter, cut into ½-inch slices

2 large egg yolks

¾ cup heavy whipping cream

FILLING

½ cup (1 stick) unsalted butter

2 tablespoons all-purpose flour

2 cups dark corn syrup

1 cup granulated sugar

3 large eggs

¼ teaspoon kosher salt

2 tablespoons bourbon (optional)

2 cups whole macadamia nuts

½ cup chocolate chips (optional)

Powdered sugar for dusting

Using an electric mixer fitted with the paddle attachment, mix the flour, salt, and sugar on low speed until combined. Add the butter to the flour mixture and mix on low speed for 1 to 1½ minutes, or until the mixture looks crumbly, with bits of dough the size of dried peas.

In a medium bowl, whisk together the egg yolks and cream, then add them to the flour mixture, mixing on low speed just until the dough is combined. Continue mixing for another 10 seconds. If the dough is too dry to form a ball, add more cream, 1 tablespoon at a time. Gently mold the dough into a disk, cover in plastic wrap, and refrigerate while you make the nut filling.

To make the filling: Preheat the oven to 350°F. Grease 3-inch muffin pans with butter or cooking spray. Melt the butter in a saucepan over medium heat and whisk in the flour. Stir in the syrup and sugar, bring the mixture to a boil, and remove the saucepan from the stove. Whisk the eggs in a large bowl just until blended. Pour ¼ cup of the hot mixture into the eggs and whisk until combined. (Mixing a small amount of the hot mixture into the eggs keeps the eggs from scrambling.) Gradually whisk the rest of the hot mixture into the eggs. Whisk in the salt and bourbon, if using.

To assemble the pies: On a lightly floured work surface, use a rolling pin to roll the dough into a ⅛-inch-thick disk. Dip a 4-inch biscuit cutter in flour and cut out rounds as close together as possible. Lightly press the rounds of dough into the muffin pans to cover the bottom and sides evenly. Spoon in the macadamia nuts, evenly dividing them among the muffin cups, and sprinkle with the chocolate chips, if using. Pour the syrup over the nuts and chocolate chips until the cups are almost full. Bake for 30 to 40 minutes, until the crust is golden brown and the filling is set. Remove from the oven and let cool in the pans for 10 minutes. Run a small spatula or knife around the edge of each pie to loosen it, then gently remove from the pan. Dust with powdered sugar just before serving.

Cookie Decorating

Little Elle Fischer, eight years old, could not stop decorating cookies. As soon as she finished, she'd start on another, intently arranging sprinkles and tiny silver dragées on red-and-green-frosted cookies. She wasn't the only one captivated by tables groaning with Christmas candies, pots of colored frosting, sprinkles, cookie cutters, rolling pins, and cookie dough. I had invited an assortment of my favorite kids, aged five to ten, for a cookie decorating party on the second-floor porch at Rather Sweet Bakery & Café. All of them—boys and girls alike—worked diligently at cutting and decorating cookies.

Beforehand, my friend and photographer Laurie Smith, a mother of young children herself, wondered if such young kids would get out of hand. I started to worry, too, thinking perhaps the idea was a big mistake. Would I end up with a bunch of unruly, sugar-crazed kids hurling cookie projectiles from our second-floor porch?

Our concerns melted as soon as the kids showed up. Their eyes widened and sparkled at the tantalizing array of candy and cookies. Although they had to work in shifts, those waiting their turn launched neither tantrums nor cookies. We all had so much fun, I'm hoping to make this an annual event.

The key to a successful cookie decorating party is advance planning and preparation.

Set up two tables, one for rolling and cutting out dough and one for decorating.

Bake at least 3 dozen cookies (page 139) in assorted shapes beforehand, so the kids can start icing and decorating right away.

You should also have at least one or two batches of chilled dough, a few rolling pins, and lots of cookie cutters so those who are not decorating can roll out cookies. Tint icing in at least three different colors. Set out tumblers filled with butter knives for spreading frosting. Fill assorted bowls with candy, colored sprinkles, and dragées. And have plenty of lightly moistened old dishcloths or paper towels handy for wiping messy hands.

Enlist several adult helpers to shuttle cookies to and from the oven, and to provide oversight in general.

Create a separate space for a hot chocolate bar (page 134) and finger food (try Chicken and Egg Checkerboard Club Sandwiches on page 135, and Fresh Veggies with Rather Sweet Ranch Dressing on page 138). Use festive paper plates and napkins for food, and assorted mugs for the hot chocolate. Leave a stack of extra paper plates and a roll of aluminum foil at each table so kids can pack up their cookies to take home. For favors, give each child a homemade lollipop (below) and an Initial Cookie (adjacent), hanging a cookie around each child's neck as he or she leaves. First-grader Isabelle Mohon, who attended the cookie decorating party as well as several other events for kids at the bakery, recently drove past Rather Sweet with her father and told him in her most serious voice: "That's where I work." I feel pretty lucky to have so many kids from the community "working" for me.

FOR THE HOT CHOCOLATE BAR: Make pitchers of heated chocolate-flavored milk and set out bowls or tumblers filled with peppermint sticks, marshmallows, and lightly sweetened whipped cream. Fill a tumbler with spoons so the kids can serve themselves.

TO MAKE THE INITIAL COOKIES: Buy alphabet cookie cutters and a length of silk cord. Let each child cut out a cookie using the letter of his or her first name. Use the end of a paintbrush to punch a hole in the top of the cookie before baking. String a cooled cookie on a piece of silk cord and knot it at the ends to make a necklace.

Rebecca's Homemade Lollipops

Seventeen magazine asked me to develop an easy candy for present-giving. These lollipops are about as easy as it gets. All you need are some lollipop molds and sticks, available at a crafts store. Holiday lollipop molds go on sale in the late fall or early winter.

Yield: 8 lollipops

2 cups sugar

¾ cup water

¼ cup light corn syrup

5 drops green, yellow, or red food coloring

2 teaspoons lime extract for green lollipops, lemon extract for yellow, or cherry extract for red

1 teaspoon freshly squeezed lemon juice

Coat 8 lollipop molds with nonstick spray and place the lollipop sticks in the molds. Combine the sugar, water, and corn syrup in an 8-cup saucepan over medium heat. Heat until the sugar dissolves, then clip a candy thermometer to the side of the pan and bring the mixture to a boil without stirring. When the candy thermometer registers 260°F, add the food coloring of choice. Do not stir; the color will disperse on its own. Continue cooking until the mixture reaches 300°F. Remove from the heat and stir in the extract of choice and the lemon juice. Be careful; the syrup is very hot. Pour the syrup into the molds and let cool until hard.

Chicken and Egg
Checkerboard Club Sandwiches

People have been requesting my egg salad recipe for years—so here it is. As a rule, we don't add the jalapeño, and we remain firmly in the less-is-more camp when it comes to mayonnaise. Too much mayo results in a wet egg salad that oozes out of the sandwich when bitten.

Once you've made the egg salad (up to 2 days ahead), this festive sandwich becomes just another assembly job. If you insist on doing it all yourself, I've provided instructions for poached chicken breasts. I'm betting—especially during the hectic holiday season—most will head for the local deli to pick up thick-sliced grilled chicken breasts. I'm all for that.

Yield: 16 triple-decker mini sandwiches

EGG SALAD

8 large eggs at room temperature

2 stalks celery, diced

2 green onions (white and green parts), finely chopped

2 tablespoons minced fresh flat-leaf parsley

2 tablespoons Dijon mustard

½ cup sweet relish, drained

½ to ¾ cup homemade (page 55) or store-bought mayonnaise

¼ teaspoon ground white pepper

¼ teaspoon kosher salt, or to taste

1 jalapeño pepper, seeded and minced (optional)

Chopped green olives (optional)

POACHED CHICKEN

4 skinless, boneless chicken breast halves

Kosher salt and freshly ground pepper to taste

4 tablespoons salted butter at room temperature

1 package thin-sliced cocktail-sized pumpernickel bread

1 package thin-sliced cocktail-sized rye bread

4 ripe Hass avocados

Juice of 1 lemon

Leaves from 1 head butter or Boston lettuce

4 small ripe tomatoes, sliced

To make the egg salad: Carefully set the eggs in a large saucepan of water. Bring to a boil, then reduce the heat to a simmer and cook for 15 minutes. Pour out the hot water and add cold water to cover the eggs. Use now, or refrigerate for no more than 1 week. Peel and coarsely chop the eggs. In a large bowl, combine the chopped eggs with the celery, green onions, parsley, mustard, relish, mayonnaise, white pepper, salt, jalapeño, and green olives.

To make the chicken: Fill a large sauté pan two-thirds full with water. Bring to a simmer and add the chicken breasts. Make sure they are completely covered with water. Cover the pan and cook over low heat for about 10 minutes, until each breast is opaque throughout.

135

Using tongs, transfer to a plate to cool. Season with salt and pepper and cut into ¼-inch-thick slices.

Spread a light coating of butter on one side of 24 slices of pumpernickel and 24 slices of rye bread. Arrange the bread slices in rows, butter side up, keeping the two types of bread separate. Peel, pit, and thinly slice the avocados lengthwise. Sprinkle with lemon juice to avoid browning. Place a lettuce leaf on what will be the bottom sandwich layer. If the lettuce leaves are too big, cut or tear them to fit the bread. Arrange a single layer of sliced chicken on the lettuce, and then place a layer of avocado on top of the chicken. Spread a layer of egg salad on a second slice of buttered bread and follow with a slice of tomato. Place the egg salad–topped bread on top of the avocado. Top the sandwich with the last slice of bread, butter side down.

Arrange the sandwiches on a platter in a checkerboard pattern, alternating the pumpernickel sandwiches with rye. Cover with lightly dampened paper towels and a layer of plastic wrap and refrigerate for up to 4 hours before serving.

TIP: Hard-boiled older eggs peel more easily than fresh ones, so make sure you don't use those fresh-laid eggs from your neighbor for this recipe. To keep the eggs from cracking while cooking, pierce one end of each eggshell with a sterilized needle or large safety pin.

Fresh Veggies with Rather Sweet Ranch Dressing

Most kids I know grew up on fresh vegetables served with a ranch dressing dip. I'll bet, too, that most think the dressing is grown in a bottle or made from a pouch of dried ingredients found on just about every grocery store shelf in America. For these deprived children, freshly made ranch dressing using only homemade ingredients doesn't exist. You can change all that, and it's simple to do. I'm betting you'll think twice before going back to the bottled brands.

Yield: About 1½ cups

1 cup homemade mayonnaise (page 55) or store-bought mayo

½ cup buttermilk

1 teaspoon freshly squeezed lemon juice

1 green onion top, thinly sliced

¼ teaspoon kosher salt

⅛ teaspoon ground white pepper

½ teaspoon dried dill weed (optional)

Baby carrots or carrot sticks, celery sticks, red bell pepper strips, sugar snap peas, and/or other favorite vegetables for dipping

Whisk the mayonnaise and buttermilk in a medium bowl until combined. Whisk in the lemon juice, green onion top, salt, pepper, and dill. Serve with the veggies of your choice.

♛ TIP: I love the color green onions give this dressing, but if you prefer, you can substitute 2 teaspoons minced shallots.

138

Grandma's Sugar Cookies

This recipe came from my friend Sam McNeely's mother-in-law, Elva Jean, a New Orleans native. The kids all call her Grandma, so Sam does, too. The baking powder makes these cookies pleasingly puffy, and fresh nutmeg gives them a delicate, distinctive flavor.

Yield: About 4 dozen cookies

½ cup (1 stick) unsalted butter at room
    temperature

1½ cups granulated sugar

2 large eggs at room temperature

1 teaspoon vanilla extract

3½ cups all-purpose flour

2 teaspoons baking powder

Pinch of kosher salt

1½ teaspoons freshly grated nutmeg

½ cup milk

BUTTER ICING

½ cup (1 stick) unsalted butter at room
    temperature

1 pound powdered sugar

4 to 6 tablespoons heavy whipping cream

1 teaspoon vanilla extract

Assorted food colorings of your choice

Using an electric mixer fitted with the paddle attachment, cream the butter on medium speed until fluffy, about 1 minute. Add the sugar and beat for another minute. Add the eggs, one at a time, beating after each addition. Add the vanilla. Stir together the flour, baking powder, salt, and nutmeg in a medium bowl. Add the flour mixture to the butter mixture in 3 increments, alternating with the milk in 2 increments, starting and ending with the flour. Form the dough into a ball, then divide in half. Cover with plastic wrap and refrigerate for at least 3 hours or up to 3 days; it may also be frozen for up to 1 month.

Preheat the oven to 375°F. Line baking sheets with parchment paper or silicone mats, or grease generously with butter or cooking spray.

Place the dough on a large piece of parchment paper lightly sprinkled with flour. Sprinkle the dough with flour. Using a floured rolling pin, roll the dough out to a ⅛-inch thickness. Cut

out the dough with cookie cutters. Using a metal spatula, place the cookies ½ inch apart on the prepared pans. Combine the dough scraps and reroll the dough to cut out more cookies. (Reroll the dough scraps only once, or the cookies will become tough from over-handling.) Bake for 8 to 10 minutes, until light golden brown around the edges. Remove from the oven and let cool for 10 minutes on the pans, then use a metal spatula to transfer to wire racks to cool completely.

To make the butter icing: Using an electric mixer fitted with the paddle attachment, cream the butter on medium speed until fluffy, about 1 minute. Add the powdered sugar and beat 1 minute more. Add 4 tablespoons of the cream and beat for 3 to 4 minutes, until the icing is fluffy and thick enough to spread. If the icing is too thick, add more whipping cream a tablespoon at a time and beat for an additional 2 minutes. Once the icing is the proper consistency, beat in the vanilla. Select food colorings and divide the icing into corresponding portions in small to medium bowls. Stir in the food coloring. Spoon each color of icing in a pastry bag fitted with the tip of your choice. (If you have no pastry bags, snip a tiny corner off of plastic sandwich bags.) Set the cookies on waxed paper and decorate with abandon.

CHAPTER FOUR

CHRISTMAS DAY

I ADORED CHRISTMAS AS A KID, because my mother always made it memorable. She would buy me one special present and have it beautifully wrapped—one was a stunning satin nightgown that made me feel like a princess. (I still have it.) But the best present I ever got was a matching pink oven and refrigerator for my backyard playhouse. Even then, I couldn't stay away from my oven.

Both my mother and my stepmother created a beautiful Christmas table. Every year, my stepmother sets a personalized Christmas ornament on each plate. Her table decorations and themes change from year to year. One year, she harvested a bumper crop of fat lemons from her patio Meyer lemon tree, so she used them to decorate her Christmas Day table. She arranged them in candle holders, teacups, and glass containers. The rest were hung on a small wire Christmas tree that served as a centerpiece.

Our family Christmas dinners haven't changed much over the years. We all vie for Green Bean Bundles (page 147), and my sister-in-law still brings sweet potato casserole (page 160). My mother's moist corn bread dressing (page 156) makes an annual appearance, and no would have it any other way. Because my mother died when I was in college, my father and stepmother were my Christmas throughout my adult years. After I divorced and became a single mother of a two-year-old, we all worked together to play Santa Claus. I remember Dad getting furious with me because I bought Frances a complicated dollhouse that took us until 4 A.M. on Christmas morning to assemble. But it didn't stop him from getting up to make the customary Christmas Day fried egg sandwich for his first grandchild. Long ago, he decided an egg sandwich was the perfect morning meal, enough to sustain but not enough to get in the way of enjoying the upcoming Christmas Day feast. Now that he is gone, there is no replacing his presence at our Christmas table.

I suppose that's why, more than ever, I feel that Christmas is a time to appreciate friends, family, and community. It's easy to do in a tight-knit town like Fredericksburg. Recently, Dr. Nancy Thomas, a local physician with training as both an internist and a pediatrician, spearheaded a drive to open a holiday skating rink with proceeds going to cystic fibrosis research. She talked to others who'd taken on similar projects throughout the country. Many tried to dissuade her, warning that a temporary rink would be too expensive for a small town like Fredericksburg. She proved them wrong. That year, the rink opened the day after Thanksgiving and was busy until the New Year, when it closed for the season. In its first year, proceeds from the rink raised about $60,000 for CF research. We expect it to be even more successful this year.

Hot Spiced Citrus Claret

Art historian and diplomat wife Trish Young presided over numerous parties during her time abroad in Asia. She shared this recipe with my coauthor, Alison Oresman, years ago. Most of the work can be done in advance, making this a natural choice for handling those inevitable holiday drop-ins. I like to make a batch in the early afternoon on Christmas Day. I keep it warm on the stove throughout the day, which infuses the house with the scent of cinnamon and cloves. I greet whomever shows up that afternoon or evening with a warm, welcoming mugful.

Becker Vineyards, located about ten miles east of Fredericksburg, makes a wonderful claret, a perfect candidate for this recipe or for drinking au naturel. Dr. Richard and Bunny Becker, who live in nearby San Antonio, have created a beautiful Hill Country vineyard. Behind the vineyard is a three-acre lavender field inspired by a trip the couple took to Provence. The annual spring Becker Vineyards lavender festival has become a destination event. Rather Sweet often partners with Becker Vineyards, providing food for wine-tasting luncheons and special events.

{ Yield: About 8 servings }

1½ cans (6 ounces each) frozen lemonade concentrate

¼ cup whole cloves

8 cinnamon sticks

1 scant cup sugar

1 gallon claret wine

2 lemons, scrubbed and sliced

2 oranges, scrubbed and sliced

2 star fruit, sliced (optional)

Bring the concentrate, cloves, cinnamon, and sugar to a boil over high heat in a large saucepan. Reduce the heat to low and simmer for 20 minutes. At this point, the syrup can be stored in a glass jar and refrigerated for up to 1 week. When ready to serve, stir the wine and syrup together in a large pot and warm over low heat. Add the sliced lemon, orange, and star fruit, if using. Use a ladle to pour the drink into mugs.

Crab in Ramekins

Lump crabmeat swathed in a creamy cheese sauce, topped with a crisp layer of bread crumbs, and served in individual ramekins makes an ideal first course. More good news: The recipe doubles easily if you are feeding a crowd, and it can be made one day ahead and baked just before serving. In fact, making the dish ahead deepens and improves its flavor. My friend Sam McNeely, a native of Louisiana, is a veteran hostess and entertaining whiz. She adapted this version from a recipe from one of Baton Rouge's premier seafood restaurants, Mike Anderson's. In 1975, Anderson, a former Louisiana State University all-American football player, opened a small "po'boy" shop and fish market near his alma mater. Business grew, and in 1982, he opened a larger, more sophisticated venue. Mike Anderson's Seafood Restaurant regularly appears on lists of the city's top seafood restaurants.

{ Yield: 4 servings }

4 tablespoons unsalted butter

2 cups chopped sweet white onions

⅓ cup chopped celery

1 teaspoon Cajun seasoning, such as Bell's

¼ cup all-purpose flour

½ teaspoon baking powder

⅛ teaspoon kosher salt

2 tablespoons shredded Gruyère cheese

¼ cup shredded Cheddar cheese

1 tablespoon grated Parmesan cheese

3 cups heavy whipping cream

1 egg yolk

1 tablespoon chopped green onion

1 pound fresh or pasteurized lump crabmeat, picked over for shell

1 cup panko (Japanese bread crumbs)

Preheat the oven to 450°F. Grease four 1-cup ramekins with butter or cooking spray. In a large, heavy saucepan, melt the butter over medium heat. Stir in the onions and celery until coated with butter. Reduce the heat to low, cover, and cook for about 15 minutes, or until the vegetables are soft. Stir in the Cajun seasoning and cook for 1 minute. Stir in the flour, baking powder, salt, and cheeses. Increase the heat to medium and cook, stirring constantly, until the cheeses melt. Whisk in 1½ cups of the cream, then the egg yolk, then the remaining 1½ cups cream. Whisk over low heat until the mixture is creamy and slightly thickened, about 5 minutes. Stir in the green onion, then gently fold in the crabmeat to avoid breaking it up.

Spoon one-fourth of the mixture into each of the prepared ramekins. The ramekins can be made ahead up to this point, covered, and refrigerated for up to 1 day. To bake, sprinkle ¼ cup panko over the top of each ramekin.

Place on a rimmed baking sheet or in a baking pan and bake for about 20 minutes, until the mixture is bubbly and the bread crumbs are golden brown. (Add about 5 minutes to the baking time if the dish has been refrigerated overnight.) Serve immediately.

👑 **TIP:** Sam says that if she were making this dish in her native Louisiana, she'd use half lump crab and half crab claw meat, because claw meat has a more intense crab flavor. If claw meat is available in your area, try it, and see whether you agree.

Green Bean Bundles

At our house, green bean bundles are the first thing to disappear from the Christmas buffet (see photo on page 151). Leftovers? Unheard of. Everyone takes at least three or four bundles to start, and that's the end of them. I suppose they would be good reheated the next day. I'll never know.

{ Yield: 6 to 8 servings }

1½ pounds green beans, trimmed
½ cup (1 stick) unsalted butter
½ teaspoon dry mustard
1 teaspoon packed brown sugar
1 clove garlic, minced
¼ teaspoon kosher salt
8 ounces bacon

Fill a large saucepan with water and bring it to a boil over high heat. Wash and trim the beans. Add the beans to the boiling water and blanch for 3 to 4 minutes, until the beans are pliable but still crunchy. Drain the beans and run them under cold water. Pat dry with paper towels or a clean dish towel and place them in a shallow ovenproof casserole. In a medium saucepan, melt the butter over medium heat. Stir in the dry mustard, brown sugar, garlic, and salt. Pour the butter mixture over the green beans, cover with plastic wrap, and refrigerate for at least 4 hours or overnight.

Preheat the oven to 375°F. Make a bundle of 8 or 9 beans, wrap half a bacon slice around each bundle, secure with a toothpick, and arrange in a single layer in the same casserole used for marinating.

Bake, uncovered, for 45 minutes, or until the bacon is cooked and the beans look wrinkled. Remove from the oven and serve warm or at room temperature.

👑 **TIP:** You can use very thin haricots verts or baby Blue Lake beans for this recipe. No need to blanch them; just wash, marinate, and bundle them up. Bake for about 35 minutes.

Baked Apple Pear Chutney

I began making this chutney with the peach bounty that overflows from local roadside stands every spring. Then winter descends and peaches are no more. So I tried the recipe with fall/winter standbys: pears and apples. Paired with Texas Spice-Rubbed Roast Pork (page 150), my seasonal chutney has become the family's newest holiday classic.

{ Yield: 6 to 8 servings }

½ cup whole pecans

1 tablespoon olive oil

1 yellow onion, chopped

1 tablespoon minced fresh ginger

1 clove garlic, minced

2 pounds unpeeled pears, cored and
    coarsely chopped

1 unpeeled Granny Smith apple, cored and
    coarsely chopped

Juice of 1 lime

1 cup good-quality white wine vinegar

½ cup granulated sugar

½ cup firmly packed brown sugar

½ teaspoon kosher salt

¼ cup dried cherries

2 tablespoons dried cranberries (optional)

1 tablespoon brandy

Preheat the oven to 350°F. Arrange the pecans on a rimmed baking sheet in a single layer and toast in the oven for 7 to 9 minutes, until darker in color and aromatic. Remove from the oven, let cool, and chop coarsely.

In a large, heavy saucepan, heat the olive oil over medium to medium-low heat. Add the onion, ginger, and garlic and sauté for about 5 minutes, until the onion is translucent. (Do not let it brown.) Stir in the pears, apple, lime juice, vinegar, sugars, salt, cherries, cranberries, and brandy. Bring to a boil, reduce the heat to medium-low, and simmer, uncovered, for about 1 hour, until the chutney is thickened, most of the vinegar has been absorbed, and the juice has a syrupy consistency. Remove from the heat and let cool, then stir in the toasted pecans. To store, cover and refrigerate for up to 1 week.

TIP: For a spectacular presentation, buy the smallest apples you can find, never mind the color. Preheat the oven to 350°F. Use a melon baller to neatly scoop out the seeds and core of each apple, starting at the stem end. Take care not to cut through the very bottom of the apple. Arrange the apples, cored side up, in the cups of a muffin pan or on a baking sheet lightly coated with cooking spray. (If using a baking sheet, cut a thin slice off the bottoms of the apples so they will remain upright while they cook.) Stuff each apple with a spoonful of chutney. Bake until the apples are soft but not falling apart, 30 to 45 minutes. Remove from the oven and serve warm or at room temperature.

Texas Spice-Rubbed Roast Pork

For several years after we adopted our pet pig, Priscilla, my daughter, Frances, outlawed pork consumption at home. How could we even think about it, with our darling porker roaming around in the backyard? But I never did give it up at the bakery. I love pork for its ease of preparation and versatility. I roast pork for fajitas, barbecue sandwiches, and just to slice and eat. Meanwhile, Priscilla can no longer be called little. (I want to be charitable—she is a beloved pet after all—so I call her condition "chubby.") If I'm not careful she eats everyone else's food, including my chickens', ducks', and dog's, all of whom share space in my tiny backyard farm. (It's hard to believe that when we first got her she slept in my tennis shoe.) Priscilla is a pig—what can I say?

{ **Yield: 6 servings, with plenty left over for sandwiches** }

1 boneless pork loin roast (5 to 6 pounds)

One 12-ounce can or bottle bock beer

¼ cup olive oil

¼ cup freshly squeezed lime juice

3 tablespoons Worcestershire sauce

2 tablespoons honey

1 tablespoon chili powder

1 teaspoon kosher salt

½ teaspoon freshly ground pepper

2 tablespoons canola oil for searing

Baked Apple Pear Chutney (page 149) for serving

Resist the urge to trim any visible fat from the pork loin. The fat will help keep the pork moist as it roasts. In a large resealable plastic bag, combine the beer, olive oil, lime juice, Worcestershire sauce, and honey. Gently submerge the pork in the marinade, seal the bag, and place in a large bowl or baking pan. Refrigerate overnight or for up to 24 hours. Remove the pork from the marinade and pour the marinade into a large measuring cup. Combine the chili powder, salt, and pepper in a small bowl. Rub it evenly over the pork.

Preheat the oven to 350°F. In a large sauté pan, heat the oil over high heat. Place the roast in the sauté pan and sear until the meat is evenly browned, 1 to 2 minutes per side. Transfer the pork to a large roasting pan, and pour half the reserved marinade around the roast. (Do not pour it over the roast, or it may wash away some of the chili rub.)

Bake for about 45 minutes, then add the rest of the marinade to the bottom of the pan. Bake another 45 minutes, or until an instant-read thermometer inserted in the center of the roast registers 140° to 145°F, for a total roasting time of about 1½ hours. Remove from the oven and let rest for 10 to 15 minutes before slicing. Serve with Green Bean Bundles (page 147) and the chutney alongside.

continued

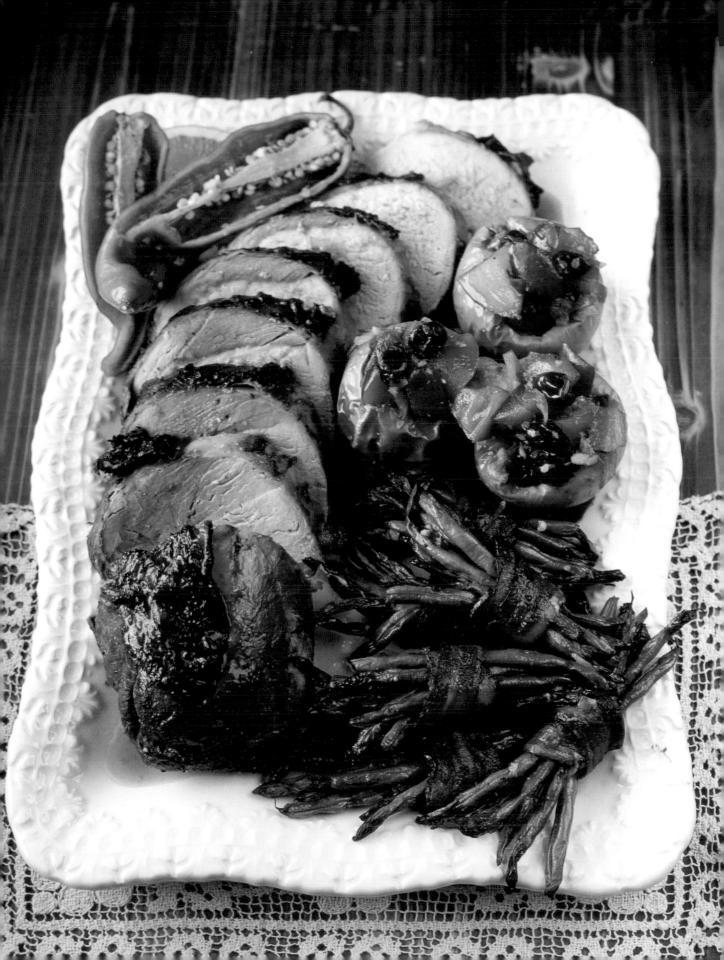

Fresh Pear and Candied-Walnut Salad with Pomegranate Vinaigrette

Christmas food can be heavy so I wanted to create a light and refreshing salad for the bakery. Marinating the pears in pomegranate juice stains them a festive pink and protects them from turning brown, and a sprinkling of candied walnuts and pomegranate seeds gives this salad a stylish finish. Substitute goat cheese for the Gorgonzola to give the salad an even lighter profile.

{ **Yield: 4 servings** }

2 pears, peeled, cored, and cut into 1-inch cubes

1 cup unsweetened pomegranate juice

Leaves from 2 heads butter lettuce

1 cup candied walnuts, pecans, or hazelnuts (see Tip), coarsely chopped

1 cup crumbled Gorgonzola cheese or fresh goat cheese

Seeds from 1 large pomegranate

VINAIGRETTE

½ shallot, thinly sliced

3 tablespoons cider vinegar

¼ cup reserved pomegranate juice, above

2 tablespoons whole-grain mustard

3 tablespoons honey

¾ cup canola oil

½ teaspoon kosher salt

Pinch of ground white pepper

In a medium bowl, marinate the pears in the pomegranate juice for at least 15 minutes. Line each of 4 salad plates with 1 or 2 lettuce leaves. Tear the rest of the lettuce leaves into bite-sized pieces. Drain the pears, reserving ¼ cup of the pomegranate marinade to make the vinaigrette. Mound one-fourth of the torn lettuce and one-fourth of the marinated pears on each salad plate. Sprinkle the nuts, Gorgonzola or goat cheese, and pomegranate seeds evenly over each salad.

To make the vinaigrette: In a small bowl, marinate the shallot in the cider vinegar for at least 5 minutes. In a food processor, combine the reserved ¼ cup pomegranate juice, mustard, honey, shallot, cider vinegar, and oil. Process until thoroughly blended. Season with salt and pepper. Drizzle the vinaigrette over each salad and serve immediately.

👑 **TIP:** Candied pecans, walnuts, or hazelnuts are widely available in most grocery stores, saving you from the hassle of making them yourself. If you don't see them on the shelves with the packaged nuts, check out the bulk foods section.

Cajun Roast Turkey

Just thinking about all the turkey-baking techniques trumpeted by newspapers, maga-zines, TV cooking shows, and well-meaning friends dying to share their latest "foolproof" method makes me tired. I'm sticking with the tried-and-true approach—with just one newfangled wrinkle: brining. I've found that brining the bird for at least twelve hours before baking makes for moist and tender meat that stands up to cooking at a steady 325°F. No need to fiddle with the oven temperature or flip the bird from breast to back halfway through roasting as though it were involved in some low-level gymnastics com-petition. All I do to season my turkey is pat it inside and out with Cajun seasoning, throw a lemon and a few garlic cloves into the body cavity, and coat it with melted but-ter. Brine, bake, and baste, and you'll be the proud bearer of a beautifully burnished unstuffed turkey on Christmas Day.

{ Yield: 8 to 10 servings, with leftovers }

BRINE

2 cups water, plus more water to cover the
   turkey

1 cup kosher salt

1 cup firmly packed brown sugar

Ice cubes for cooling

One 12- to 14-pound turkey

1 onion, quartered

2 tablespoons Cajun seasoning

1 lemon, halved

3 to 4 cloves garlic, peeled

1 cup (2 sticks) unsalted butter

½ cup all-purpose flour

To make the brine: In a large saucepan, com-bine the 2 cups water, salt, and sugar and set over high heat. Cook, stirring, until the salt and sugar are completely melted. Fill the saucepan with ice cubes to quickly cool the brine. Put the turkey in a large stockpot, heavy plastic bag, or cooler large enough to hold the bird when covered. Add enough cold water to cover the turkey. Add the cooled brine and the onion. Add more ice if you are brining the turkey in a cooler. (The advantage of a cooler is there's no need to find refrigerator space.) If brining in a stockpot or plastic bag, place in the refrigerator. Leave the turkey in the brine for at least 12 hours or up to 24 hours.

To bake the turkey: Preheat the oven to 325°F. Remove the turkey from the brine, rinse under cool water in the sink, and pat dry with paper towels. Place it on a greased V-shaped roast-ing rack in a large roasting pan. Pat the Cajun seasoning evenly all over the turkey, inside and out. Place the lemon and garlic in the turkey's body cavity. In a small saucepan, melt the but-ter over low heat. Stir the flour into the melted butter and pour it over the turkey, taking care to cover the whole bird. Bake the turkey, bast-ing about every 30 minutes, for 3 to 4 hours. (I know basting is a hassle, but think of it as just another part of the holiday ritual.) The turkey is done when the legs are loose in their sockets and an instant-read thermometer stuck in the thickest part of the thigh without touching bone registers 175° to 180°F. Remove from the oven and let rest for about 30 minutes before carving.

TIP: Although versions differ, Cajun seasoning is a lightly spicy mixture of salt, paprika, cayenne pepper, black pepper, and seasonings such as garlic or onion powder. Most grocery stores throughout the country carry at least one variety.

TIP: A word about giblets—people either love them or hate them. I am firmly in the "love them" camp. (I think I inherited the giblet-loving gene from my mom.) To prepare the giblets—the liver, heart, and gizzard—brown them, along with the neck, in about 1 tablespoon oil in a hot skillet over medium-high heat. Fill a medium saucepan three-fourths full with cool water, add the giblets, cover, and simmer over low heat for about 1 hour. Drain, reserving the broth, and finely chop the gizzard, heart, and neck. (I only use the liver to flavor the broth, not as an addition to gravy or dressing.) Stir them into My Mother's Best Corn Bread Dressing (page 156) just before baking or add them to your turkey gravy. Use the turkey broth for gravy or dressing.

155

My Mother's Best Corn Bread Dressing

This corn bread dressing is my all-time Christmas dinner favorite. After my mother passed away, I made the dressing every Christmas. Now, my stepmother is kind enough to carry on the tradition for our family Christmas feasts.

Included in the little notebook of recipes my mother left for me is this note about dressing: "Making the bread mixture very moist is what makes a good dressing." I have made one change to her recipe. She used Pioneer corn bread mix in her dressing. I've substituted a homemade corn bread made in a cast-iron skillet. If you wish, substitute commercial corn bread crumbs, which appear on most grocery store shelves at the beginning of the holiday season.

{ Yield: About 7 cups; 8 to 10 servings, with leftovers }

CORN BREAD

1½ cups stone-ground cornmeal (medium grind)

¾ cup all-purpose flour

1½ teaspoons kosher salt

2¼ teaspoons baking powder

2 tablespoons sugar

3 large eggs

1½ cups milk

7 tablespoons canola oil

DRESSING

2 slices bacon

1¼ cups chopped onions

1¼ cups chopped celery

½ red bell pepper, seeded, deveined, and diced

½ green bell pepper, seeded, deveined, and diced

2 cloves garlic, minced

4 tablespoons unsalted butter

½ teaspoon dried sage

½ teaspoon poultry seasoning

½ teaspoon Cajun seasoning

1 bunch green onions, including green parts, chopped

3 cups coarsely crumbled corn bread, above

3 cups day-old white bread, torn into pieces

2 large eggs, lightly beaten

4 cups turkey or chicken stock

Chopped cooked giblets (optional)

To make the corn bread: Preheat the oven to 375°F. In a large bowl, stir together the cornmeal, flour, salt, baking powder, and sugar. In a medium bowl, whisk together the eggs, milk, and 6 tablespoons of the canola oil. Pour the egg mixture into the cornmeal mixture and stir just until incorporated.

Grease an 8-inch cast-iron or other heavy ovenproof skillet with the remaining 1 tablespoon oil. Preheat the skillet in the hot oven for about 5 minutes. Pour the batter into the skillet and bake for 25 to 30 minutes, until

the corn bread is firm to the touch and lightly brown on top. Unmold the corn bread onto a wire rack and let cool completely.

To make the dressing: Preheat the oven to 350°F. Grease a 10 by 15-inch baking dish with butter or cooking spray.

In a medium skillet, cook the bacon over medium heat until crisp. Using tongs, transfer the bacon to a plate and reserve for another use. Add 1 cup of the chopped onions, 1 cup of the chopped celery, and all of the peppers and garlic to the bacon fat and sauté until soft, about 5 minutes. Add the butter; when completely melted, stir in the sage, poultry seasoning, and Cajun seasoning. Remove the skillet from the heat and stir in the green onions and the remaining ¼ cup onion and ¼ cup celery.

In a large bowl, mix together the corn bread and white bread. Add the sautéed vegetables and stir until combined. Lightly stir the eggs and stock into the bread mixture until evenly incorporated. As my mother says, the dressing ought to be very moist.

Place in the prepared baking dish and bake for about 1 hour, until lightly browned. Serve immediately. Well-wrapped leftover dressing can be refrigerated for up to 3 days.

♛ **TIP:** It may be hard to believe, but leftover stuffing makes a wonderful post-Christmas sandwich. Use your favorite bread, slather on a layer of cranberry sauce, pile on some stuffing, and chow down.

Day-after-Christmas Cajun Turkey Gumbo

Thrifty cooks know that the holiday turkey carcass can be simmered in water and reborn as the base for flavor-packed soups or stews. With this recipe, you can transform it into a rich gumbo, the classic Creole stew. (Dispatch any leftover gravy by adding it as well.)

The first step is to make a roux, a mixture of equal parts flour and fat cooked over low heat; this thickens the gumbo and is a mainstay of Cajun and Creole cooking. My Louisiana-born friend and Cajun-cooking expert Sam McNeely suggests making a large batch, which can be refrigerated for up to 2 weeks or frozen for up to 2 months. This makes sense, given the long stirring time it takes to bring the flour-fat mixture to the desired color and doneness. Sam describes the color changes in roux as it cooks: "the ecru stage, then the peanut butter stage, and then the final red-chocolate stage," which imparts the distinctive flavor to gumbo. "The whole point of roux is to brown the flour without burning it," Sam says. "You can only get to that point by stirring constantly the entire time it cooks." Both Sam and I use a traditional cast-iron skillet to make roux, but any heavy skillet will do, such as those manufactured by Le Creuset, Emile Henry, or All-Clad.

{ Yield: About 8 servings }

ROUX

- 2 cups canola oil
- 2 cups all-purpose flour

TURKEY STOCK

- 1 leftover turkey carcass
- 1 large carrot, cut into thirds
- 1 large onion, quartered
- 2 stalks celery, cut into 2-inch pieces
- 1 tablespoon peppercorns
- 1 dried bay leaf

- 1½ cups white and wild or brown rice blend (I like Lundberg Wild Blend, available at many grocery stores)
- 2 large links andouille sausage (smoked, spicy pork sausage), optional
- 2 tablespoons canola oil
- 2 cups chopped yellow onions
- 2 cloves garlic, minced
- 2 bunches green onions, including green parts, thinly sliced
- 2 teaspoons Cajun seasoning
- One 14-ounce can tomatoes with green chiles
- Leftover turkey gravy (optional)
- Two 10-ounce packages frozen okra
- ¾ cup chopped fresh flat-leaf parsley
- Diced leftover turkey (optional)

To make the roux: In a large, heavy skillet or Dutch oven, combine the oil and flour. Cook over medium-low heat, stirring constantly, until the flour turns a dark chocolate brown, about 40 minutes. Remove from the heat and continue stirring for another 7 minutes. (The heat of the pan will continue the cooking process.) Reserve 1 cup for the gumbo. Spoon the rest, 1 cup at a time, into individual heavy freezer bags and refrigerate or freeze for later use.

To make the turkey stock: Place the turkey carcass in a large stockpot and add water to cover. Add the carrot, onion, celery stalks, peppercorns, and bay leaf. Cover and bring to a boil, then reduce the heat to very low and simmer for at least 4 hours, or overnight, until the bones are falling apart. Strain the broth, refrigerate it until cold, skim off the fat that congeals at the top, and reserve 4 cups for the gumbo. Cover and refrigerate for up to 3 days or freeze for up to 1 month.

Prepare the rice according to the package directions and keep warm. (The gumbo will be served over the rice.) Cut the sausage into bite-sized pieces. In a large skillet over medium heat, cook the sausage until browned, about 10 minutes. Drain the sausage on paper towels.

In a large Dutch oven or heavy pot, heat the oil over medium heat and add the onions, garlic, and green onions. Sauté until the vegetables are soft, about 5 minutes. Stir in the Cajun seasoning, 1 cup roux, 4 cups stock, tomatoes, and leftover gravy, if using. Bring to a boil, then reduce the heat and simmer for 15 to 20 minutes. Add the cooked sausage, okra, parsley, and turkey, and cook until the okra is heated through. Serve in large bowls, over the warm rice.

TIP: This recipe makes 4 cups of roux; you will have 3 cups left over for other dishes. If you don't have a handy leftover turkey carcass for making homemade stock, don't sweat it; just use 4 cups of your favorite store-bought broth.

My Sister-in-Law's Candied Sweet Potato Casserole

We've been eating these fabulous sweet potatoes since my brother Carl married Bea in 1979. Bea always makes them and brings them to our holiday feasts. In fact, for our Christmas meals, everyone has his or her deal. I do the bread and desserts. My stepmother does the roast turkey (page 154) and corn bread dressing (page 156), and my niece brings the Green Bean Bundles (page 147). We taught her to make them when she married my nephew.

Bea lists the prep time as "very little, if you don't dawdle," and the yield as "depends on your ravenous appetite."

{ **Yield: 6 servings** }

4 to 6 medium-to-large orange-fleshed
   sweet potatoes

⅔ cup granulated sugar

4 tablespoons unsalted butter, melted

2 large eggs

¼ teaspoon vanilla extract

TOPPING

1 cup firmly packed light brown sugar

⅓ cup all-purpose flour

⅓ cup unsalted butter, melted

Pinch of ground cinnamon

1 cup pecans, finely chopped

¼ cup candied ginger, finely chopped

Preheat the oven to 425°F. Line a baking sheet with aluminum foil. Pierce the sweet potatoes several times with a fork or paring knife, and bake them on the prepared pan for 1 hour, or until tender. Remove from the oven and let cool for about 15 minutes, until cool to the touch.

Reduce the oven temperature to 350°F. Coat a 9 by 13-inch baking dish with butter or cooking spray.

In a medium bowl, combine the sugar, butter, eggs, and vanilla. Using an electric mixer, beat on medium speed until creamy. Cut the potatoes in half, scoop the flesh out of the skins, and put it into a large bowl. Pour the sugar mixture into the potatoes and beat on medium speed until combined. Spoon the potatoes evenly into the prepared baking dish.

To make the topping: In a medium bowl, stir together the sugar, flour, butter, cinnamon, pecans, and candied ginger. Evenly sprinkle the potatoes with the topping and bake for about 30 minutes.

♕ **TIP:** Is it a yam or a sweet potato, and should you really care? Much confusion arises when it comes to the difference between sweet potatoes and yams. There is a difference, and it is almost certain that, regardless of its label, the tuber you'll encounter in most American grocery stores is a sweet potato. True yams grow only in tropical areas, and you're likely to find them only in Latin American specialty stores. The confusion arises, in part, because sweet potatoes come in several varieties and colors, and the deep orange, sweeter variety is often labeled a yam. (The canned sweetened ones also often are called yams, although they are sweet potatoes, too.) So don't worry about the label; just try to find ones with a dark-orange flesh.

Margie's Christmas Squash

A stellar, simple alternative for those who want a change from holiday sweet potato casseroles. The recipe comes from my old Houston pal Margie French. Our mothers were friends, and later Margie and I were young mothers together in Houston. My daughter, Frances, and I spent many a Christmas Eve at Margie's home. Then we'd all pile in the car and head to midnight Mass. A diminutive blond ball of fire, Margie is now vice president of development at the University of Texas at Dallas. She still serves this dish at Christmas because "the kids all love it." Obviously, the fact that her children are all grown up hasn't diminished their affection for Christmas Squash.

{ Yield: 4 to 6 servings }

2 large acorn squash, halved and seeded

2 large eggs, lightly beaten

1 tablespoon vanilla extract

½ cup sugar

½ cup (1 stick) unsalted butter, melted

2 tablespoons all-purpose flour

½ teaspoon kosher salt

1 tablespoon baking powder

Freshly grated nutmeg to taste

Preheat the oven to 375°F. Grease an 8-cup baking dish with butter or cooking spray. Place the squash halves, cut side down, in a roasting pan. Put the pan in the oven and add water to reach ¼ inch up the sides of the pan. Bake for 1 hour, or until the squash is tender.

Remove the squash from the pan and let it cool for about 15 minutes before scooping the flesh out of the skin. In a medium bowl, combine the squash, eggs, vanilla, sugar, and butter. Using an electric mixer fitted with the paddle attachment, beat the squash mixture on medium until well blended. In a small bowl, combine the flour, salt, and baking powder. Add the flour mixture to the squash mixture and beat on medium speed until combined. Spoon into the prepared dish and top with a sprinkling of nutmeg. Bake for 30 to 45 minutes, until golden brown. Serve hot.

Grandma Wyche's Gingerbread

I copied this into my high-school cooking notebook years ago, but never tried it. As with many of these old recipes, I have no idea where my grandma got it—likely an old cookbook or newspaper article. The recipe calls for vegetable shortening—I substituted butter. In addition, her recipe called for "syrup," which I assumed meant molasses.

I am delighted with this version, which makes a beautiful, puffed cake. Although it will keep for a few days, I say gingerbread is at its very best eaten warm from the oven.

I got the idea for the hard sauce from my coauthor, Alison, when she told me her mother always served it over warm gingerbread. It's called hard sauce not for the hard liquor that many like to add, but because it must be chilled to make the butter hard before serving. I love the delicious contrast of the cold, sweetened butter melding with the warm, fragrant gingerbread.

{ Yield: 8 to 10 servings }

½ cup (1 stick) unsalted butter at room temperature

½ cup sugar

2 large eggs

2½ cups all-purpose flour

2 teaspoons ground cinnamon

4 teaspoons ground ginger

1½ teaspoons baking powder

½ teaspoon baking soda

1½ teaspoons kosher salt

⅓ cup molasses

1 cup boiling water

HARD SAUCE

½ cup (1 stick) unsalted butter at room temperature

3 cups powdered sugar

1 teaspoon vanilla extract

1 tablespoon dark rum (optional)

Preheat the oven to 350°F. Grease a 9 by 13-inch pan with butter or cooking spray.

Combine the butter and sugar in the large bowl of an electric mixer fitted with the paddle attachment. Cream on medium-high speed until light and fluffy, about 3 minutes. Add the eggs, one at a time, beating for about 30 seconds after each addition. In a large bowl, combine the flour, cinnamon, ginger, baking powder, baking soda, and salt. In a small bowl, stir the molasses into the boiling water.

Add the flour mixture to the butter mixture in 3 increments, alternating with the molasses mixture in 2 increments, starting and ending with the flour mixture. Pour the batter into the prepared pan. Bake for 20 to 25 minutes, until the cake pulls slightly away from the pan and a toothpick inserted in the center comes out clean. Remove from the oven and let cool in the pan for about 30 minutes before serving.

To make the hard sauce: Using an electric mixer fitted with the paddle attachment, beat the butter in a medium bowl on medium-high speed until light and fluffy. Add the sugar, 1 cup at a time, beating on medium-high speed until thoroughly combined. Add the vanilla and rum and beat until combined. Cover and refrigerate until ready to serve.

TIP: If you wish, press the hard sauce into silicone butter molds and refrigerate overnight. Pop them out onto individual servings of warm gingerbread.

Chocolate Cookie Crusted Eggnog Cheesecake

Here's one of my biggest, boldest, richest cheesecakes, all dressed up for the holidays with a buttery chocolate crust and a delicious eggnog filling. It's perfect for using up the leftover eggnog from your last holiday party, and perfectly fabulous to serve as a finale after Christmas dinner. It must be made a day ahead, but it's easier to make it three or four days ahead. Your Christmas will be that much more relaxed.

{ Yield: 14 to 16 servings }

CRUST

About 40 cream-filled chocolate cookies

6 tablespoons unsalted butter, melted

FILLING

Four 8-ounce packages cream cheese
(32 ounces total) at room temperature

1 cup sugar

2 large eggs

1 large egg yolk

1 cup sour cream

1¾ cups homemade (page 9) or
high-quality commercial eggnog

1 teaspoon freshly grated nutmeg

¼ teaspoon kosher salt

To make the crust: Preheat the oven to 350°F. Grease a 10-inch springform pan with an even coating of cooking spray. Wrap a single sheet of aluminum foil around the bottom and sides of the pan to prevent leakage.

In a food processor, pulse the cookies to make coarse crumbs (about 3¾ cups). Transfer the cookie crumbs to a large bowl and stir in the melted butter until combined. Firmly press the crumb mixture into the prepared pan to cover the bottom and about three-fourths of the way up the sides. (Don't mess around trying to make a perfectly straight edge—it looks quite lovely with uneven, wavy sides.)

To make the filling: Using an electric mixer fitted with the paddle attachment, beat the cream cheese and sugar in a large bowl on medium-high speed until light and fluffy, about 2 minutes. (After the first minute, stop the mixer, scrape down the cream cheese mixture with a rubber spatula, and continue beating.) Add the eggs one at a time, then the egg yolk, beating on medium-low speed after each addition until combined. Add the sour cream and eggnog separately, beating on low speed after each addition. Stir in the nutmeg and salt.

Pour the batter into the crumb-lined pan. Set the pan in a larger baking pan and place it in the oven. Use a teakettle to pour enough boiling water into the baking pan to reach halfway up the sides of the springform pan. Bake for

continued

165

about 1 hour and 30 minutes, until the filling is set around the edges but jiggles slightly in the middle; the edges should be a light golden brown. Remove from the oven and let cool on a wire rack for about 30 minutes, then refrigerate for at least 12 hours or up to 4 days.

👑 **TIP:** Recent health warnings about the risks of consuming partially hydrogenated oils have turned me into an avid reader of ingredient lists. Standard-issue chocolate cream-filled cookies often contain the offending oils. Look in the natural section of your grocery store to find brands that do not contain partially hydrogenated oils.

Carlton's Chocolate Chewies

My father was always after me to come up with a recipe for these cookies (see photo on page 164). He used to buy them from a bakery in Beaumont owned by Janey Phelan, my favorite junior-high home economics teacher. Dad would say, "If you could just make that cookie, you could make a fortune." I never got around to it. Finally, while writing this book, I took my dad's advice. I experimented until I came up with a recipe that I think is pretty close to the one he loved. I'm heartbroken that he is no longer around to enjoy it. This one's for you, Dad, and now your name is on it.

This is a great recipe for those who have diet restrictions—it's gluten free, and if you omit the nuts (see the variation), it's fat free, too.

{ Yield: About 4 dozen cookies }

2 cups whole pecans

3 large egg whites

2¼ cups powdered sugar

6 tablespoons good-quality unsweetened cocoa powder

Pinch of kosher salt

½ teaspoon vanilla extract

Preheat the oven to 350°F. Arrange the pecans on a rimmed baking sheet in a single layer and toast them for 7 to 9 minutes, until darker in color and aromatic. Remove from the oven, transfer to a bowl, let cool, and coarsely chop.

Reduce the oven temperature to 300°F. Line baking sheets with parchment paper or silicone mats.

In a large bowl, briskly whisk the egg whites until foamy, about 30 seconds. Stir in the powdered sugar, cocoa, salt, vanilla, and pecans. Using a 1-inch-diameter scoop, drop spoonfuls of dough 1½ inches apart on the prepared pans. Bake for 8 to 10 minutes, until set and shiny, with zigzag cracks on top. Remove from the oven and let cool on the pans for 5 to 10 minutes. Using a metal spatula, transfer the cookies to wire racks to cool completely. The

cookies will keep for up to 1 week in an airtight container or 3 weeks tightly wrapped and frozen.

RATHER SWEET VARIATION

This cookie is amazingly adaptable and can handle up to two additional ingredients. I have tried numerous add-ins. My favorites are 1 cup quartered dried cherries, 1 cup sweetened shredded coconut, and 1 cup semisweet chocolate chips. Nut haters can leave out the pecans, substitute one or two of the add-ins, and make the cookies as directed above.

TIP: To skip the hassle of separating egg whites from yolks, especially if you have no plans to use the leftover yolks, look in the dairy case of your local natural foods store for small containers of pure egg whites. One egg white equals about ⅛ cup. Do not use egg substitute, which is formulated with added fat to simulate an egg without cholesterol.

Wrapping Up the Holidays with Edible Gifts

Everyone loves getting edible gifts during the holidays, and half the fun of giving them is wrapping them in creative, appealing ways. Beginning in November, I'm on the lookout for singular, inexpensive packaging materials whereever I happen to be, from discount stores and antiques shops to flea markets and garage sales. And don't forget packaging specialty stores, crafts stores, or the stuff you stashed in the back of your closet after you didn't get around to using it last year (or the year before). I recently stumbled on a stack of unused Chinese-style takeout boxes decorated with pictures of Christmas holly. I bought them a few years ago meaning to fill them with, uh—I can't remember what. They are ideal for packaging homemade candies, like Denise's Vanilla Caramels (page 178).

In this section, I've included recipes for some of my favorite tasty holiday giveaways and added some tempting ways to dress up these edible presents. Start by collecting an assortment of tools and colorful materials for creating gorgeous gift packages.

ASSORTED RIBBONS AND RAFFIA: Shop the after-Christmas sales to get great deals on holiday ribbon for next year's gifts. And look for inexpensive, distinctive ribbons and raffia at crafts stores and discount stores. Keep them in a designated box and store them near your Christmas ornaments. (That way, you won't forget they are there, and you can bring them out when you decorate your tree.) Don't be afraid to recycle the best of the ribbon tied around gifts you've received throughout the year. I keep a small plastic bag in a kitchen drawer and stash my neatly folded used ribbons there for that special gift that needs a one-of-a-kind touch. Mix and match ribbons and tie them together, or twist a strand of rustic raffia with a contrasting piece of ribbon to make a memorable and attractive bow.

RAID YOUR CHILDREN'S RUBBER STAMP COLLECTION: Head to the local party or stationery store to pick up holiday stamps and a set of letter stamps and stamp pads. Buy large plain tags and personalize each gift with the recipients' names or initials, the name of the recipe you're giving, or cooking instructions. Decorate butcher paper or plain brown wrapping paper, available at discount stores and mail stores, by rubber-stamping it with holiday symbols, such as trees, Santas, stars, or candy canes.

BUY AND COLLECT COOKIE TINS: Wash and store cookie tins left over from cookies or holiday candies. Watch for deals on empty cookie tins at discount stores, and buy them as soon as you see them. They often disappear early in the season. Fill cookie tins with homemade cookies or candy, tie with a ribbon, attach a tag, and you're done.

START SAVING PRETTY JARS AND THEIR LIDS: Before you pitch empty glass jam jars, dessert topping jars, or other assorted condiment jars, check them out to see if they'd look good stocked with an edible holiday gift. Wash them well, soak off the labels, and save them to fill with Christmas goodies. Or buy small canning jars, which often are available in grocery stores, especially around the holidays.

SMALL ORNAMENTS, CANDY CANES, COOKIE CUTTERS, AND TINY LIQUOR BOTTLES: Attaching any of these with ribbon or string to an edible present adds a touch of whimsy and fun.

PINKING SHEARS AND PARCHMENT PAPER: These can be a wrapper's best friends. Use pinking shears to cut homemade gift tags or cards, a surefire way to gussie up plain Jane materials. Buy large sheets of parchment paper at kitchen stores, decorate with rubber stamps, place your edible gift in the center, gather up the corners, and tie it all together with ribbon. Use parchment paper cut with pinking shears to separate layers of cookies in a cookie tin or to make name bands to slip over homemade breads and cakes (see Aunt Milbry's Fruitcake, page 28).

Rosa's Tamales with Tomatillo Sauce

Tamales are a Mexican Christmas tradition, and they make great gifts, especially when wrapped in bags made of muslin or cheesecloth and stitched together on three sides with black or red thread. Tie with a string attached to a tag with cooking instructions and pair with a small jar of tomatillo sauce. Use pinking shears to cut a round of fabric large enough to fit over the top and sides of the jar's lid and tie it on with a ribbon or twine. And don't forget to let your friends know that your tamales are the real deal: The following recipe has been used by the Albiter family of Mexico City for at least three generations.

Tamale making is a family affair for the Albiter sisters. Just before Christmas, they gather to spend the day making tamales—about ten dozen at once—from this recipe that they learned from their mother and grandmother in their native Mexico City. Rosa Albiter Espinoza, her two sisters, Marcela Albiter and Romelia Arias, her sister-in-law, Beatriz Albiter, and Beatriz's sister-in-law, Blanca Aguirre, all work at Rather Sweet. (So do Beatriz's husband, Tomás, and the Albiter sisters' uncle, Bertine Jaramillo.) I don't know what I'd do without them. They take care of just about everything that has to do with day-to-day cooking, baking, the assembling of lunch orders, and keeping the bakery spotless.

Rosa says her mother and grandmother let her graduate from just watching to making tamales when she was ten. Now a mother of two children herself, she claims her mother's tamales are still the best.

According to Rosa, the secret to good tamales is working the dough long enough to make it smooth. Masa that has been undermixed turns tough when steamed, she says. She also warns against skimping on the meat filling. "Some people like to put a lot of masa and a little meat. That's not a tamale."

It takes time and practice to make tamales, so it makes sense to invite a few friends over and make a day of it. Once they have been wrapped in corn husks, tamales can be wrapped in plastic or aluminum foil and frozen for up to 1 month. A present of a dozen tamales and a jar of homemade tomatillo sauce means a night free from kitchen duty. Who wouldn't appreciate that?

Yield: 4 dozen tamales

FILLING

- 4 cups water
- 1 whole 3- to 4-pound chicken, cut into 8 pieces
- ½ yellow onion, cut into quarters
- 8 garlic cloves, peeled
- 1 tablespoon plus 1 teaspoon kosher salt

TOMATILLO SAUCE

- 20 tomatillos (about 2½ pounds), husked and rinsed
- 1 jalapeño pepper
- ¼ cup plus ⅓ cup olive oil
- ½ yellow onion, sliced
- 5 cloves garlic, peeled
- ½ teaspoon kosher salt

1½ teaspoons freshly ground pepper

Pinch of ground cumin

Leaves from 3 cilantro sprigs

MASA

One 6-ounce package dried corn husks

8 cups finely ground masa harina, made especially for tamales

1 tablespoon kosher salt

1 pound lard, vegetable shortening, or unsalted butter, melted

6 cups chicken stock

To make the filling: In a large stockpot, combine the water, chicken, onion, garlic, and salt. Cover and bring to a boil over high heat; then simmer until tender, about 40 minutes. Using tongs, transfer the chicken to a large bowl and let cool to the touch. Strain the broth from the stockpot into a large measuring cup. (The stock will be used to make the masa.) Skin the chicken and shred the meat into bite-sized pieces. Refrigerate in a medium bowl until you are ready to use it for the filling.

To make the tomatillo sauce: In a large stockpot, combine the tomatillos and jalapeño and fill the pot with 12 cups water. Bring to a boil over high heat, reduce the heat to medium, cover, and simmer for about 25 minutes, until the tomatillos are soft. Meanwhile, in a large sauté pan, heat the ¼ cup olive oil over medium-high heat. Add the onion and garlic and sauté, stirring occasionally, for about 10 minutes, until lightly browned. Stir in the salt, pepper, and cumin and cook for 1 minute more.

When the tomatillos are done, pour off about 8 cups of the water, leaving the remainder in the pot. In a food processor, process the tomatillos and remaining water until smooth. Add the sautéed onion mixture and process until smooth. Pour the ⅓ cup olive oil into a large stockpot, add the tomatillo purée and cilantro, and bring to a boil over high heat. Immediately remove the sauce from the heat. It can be poured into a clean container and refrigerated for up to 3 days or frozen for up to 1 month.

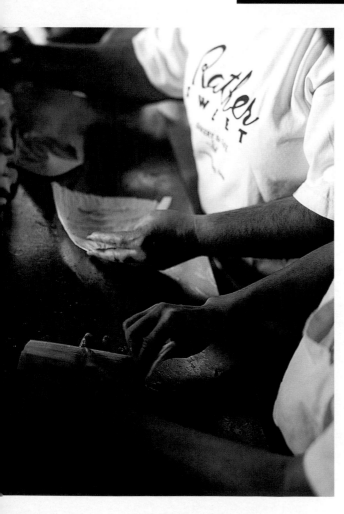

To make the masa: In a medium bowl, combine the corn husks with warm water to cover. Let soak while you prepare the masa. Combine the masa and salt in a large bowl. Pour in the melted lard and mix with a wooden spoon until the dough is cool to the touch. Use your hands to mix the dough, making sure to sweep all around the bowl to evenly incorporate all of the ingredients. Mix in this way for at least 5 minutes. (I know this is tiring, but think of it as a substitute for that aerobics class the holiday madness has forced you to forgo.) Add the chicken broth and continue mixing for another 5 minutes. (Check your heart rate. See what I mean about the aerobics class?) The masa should be soft, thick, and not at all sticky. It may taste salty, but don't worry; some of the salt will dissipate as the tamales steam.

To assemble the tamales: Set a steamer basket in a large pot and fill it with water so that it barely touches the bottom of the steamer. Remove the corn husks from the soaking water and pat them dry. Pour 1½ cups tomatillo sauce into the shredded chicken and stir until combined. Pinch off a 2-inch piece of masa and roll it into a ball in your hands.

On a work surface, smooth out a corn husk with the wide end nearest you. Press the masa ball into the middle of the husk, using your fingers to stretch it into a disk, about ⅛ inch thick and 3 inches in diameter. Leave at least a 1-inch border around the edges of the corn husk. Place a heaping tablespoonful of the chicken mixture in the middle of the masa. Fold the long side of the corn husk over onto the masa and press to gently seal.

Roll the corn husk into a cylinder, allowing the end facing toward you to be slightly thicker than the narrow end of the husk. Fold the narrow end of the husk under and set it on a plate. The wide end will be open. Repeat until all of the tamales are assembled.

Bring the water in the steamer to a simmer. Stack the tamales in the steamer basket, seam side down and open ends facing toward the center. You can stack as many layers of tamales as your pot will accommodate. Place the basket in the steamer, cover, and cook for 45 minutes. Check the water level every 20 minutes or so to ensure it has not simmered away. Fill as needed. Using tongs, remove a tamale, open it and partly peel away the corn husk. If the masa does not stick to the husk, it is done. If not done, simmer the tamales a few more minutes.

Reheat the tomatillo sauce. Serve the tamales warm or at room temperature, with a bowl of the sauce alongside for spooning over the tamales. (The tamales also can be wrapped individually in plastic wrap and refrigerated for up to 3 days or frozen for up to 1 month.)

Butter Meringue Nuts

These make distinctive Christmas gifts for teachers, friends, or neighbors. Buy attractive, inexpensive holiday mugs or glass bowls and fill them with these sweetly addicting nuts. Set each bowl in the center of a large square of plastic wrap, gather the wrap in a bunch on top of the container, and tie the wrap together with a colorful ribbon. Add a gift tag. For an even more inexpensive alternative, pack the nuts in small cellophane bags, tie with ribbon, and add a gift tag.

Patricia Oresman, my coauthor's mother, used to make these nuts every Christmas season; she'd pack them in clean mayonnaise jars, cover the screw-on tops with decorative holiday tape, and give them out to friends and family. She lost the original recipe years ago, but believes she cut it out of a magazine sometime in the early sixties. As soon as I tried them, I was hooked. These days, blanched almonds, which used to come in cellophane packages and always popped up on grocery shelves around November, can be difficult to find. I've had the best luck finding them in the bulk foods section of natural foods stores.

Yield: About 8 cups

4 cups (16 ounces) whole pecans

2 cups (8 ounces) blanched almonds

½ cup (1 stick) salted butter

2 large egg whites

Dash of kosher salt

1 cup sugar

Preheat the oven to 325°F. Spread the nuts on a large rimmed baking sheet and toast them until lightly brown and fragrant, 7 to 9 minutes. Transfer the nuts to a large bowl.

Place the butter on the rimmed baking sheet and return it to the oven to melt. In the bowl of an electric mixer fitted with the whisk attachment, beat the egg whites until stiff peaks form. Add the salt, then beat the sugar into the egg mixture about ¼ cup at a time. Gently stir the nuts into the meringue mixture.

Evenly spread the nut mixture on the baking sheet with the melted butter. Bake for 30 minutes, stirring every 10 minutes to ensure that the butter is evenly distributed among all of the nuts. The nuts are done when all of the butter has been absorbed and the meringue coating is a light brown. Remove from the oven and let cool completely. Store the nuts in an airtight container for up to 1 week.

Cheese Crispies

*Another little 1950s gem from my mother. "They make marvelous Christmas presents
and they are nice to have with drinks," she wrote. She also noted that the recipe can be
doubled with ease, and that "these freeze beautifully." Stack them in cellophane bags
tied with a ribbon, or nestle them in any holiday container that catches your fancy. I
found little Christmas pails with green handles at a going-out-of-business sale.*

Yield: About 11 dozen crackers

2½ cups (12 ounces) shredded sharp
　　Cheddar cheese

1¼ cups (2½ sticks) unsalted butter at
　　room temperature

2¼ cups all-purpose flour

½ teaspoon cayenne pepper

½ teaspoon kosher salt

2 cups puffed rice cereal

Preheat the oven to 375°F. Line baking sheets
with parchment paper or silicone mats, or
grease generously with butter or cooking
spray.

In the large bowl of an electric mixer fitted
with the paddle attachment, mix the cheese
and butter together on medium speed. Add 2
cups of the flour, the pepper, and ¼ teaspoon
of the salt and mix until well combined. Add
the cereal and use your hands to combine it
thoroughly with the flour mixture. (The electric mixer will crush the cereal too much.)
Combine the remaining ¼ cup flour and the
remaining ¼ teaspoon salt in a medium bowl.
Use your hands to roll the dough into balls
about the size of fresh cherries. Place the balls
on the prepared baking sheet. Dip the tines of
a dinner fork into the flour mixture and press
each ball down with the fork. Bake for 10 to
12 minutes, until light golden brown. Remove
from the oven and transfer to wire racks to
cool. The crackers will keep in an airtight container for up to 1 week or frozen for up to 1
month.

Denise's Vanilla Caramels

Wrapping these caramels individually in squares of waxed paper and twisting the ends closed means these don't have to be given away in covered containers. They can be mounded in small candy dishes or holiday glassware or stemware and handed out. Old-fashioned Christmas cardboard boxes, which I discovered at an antiques store, were one of my best finds this year. I filled them with caramels and gave them away to rave reviews. I have also been known to save empty animal cracker boxes and fill them with wrapped candies.

Former employee Denise Carey gave me this recipe, which she says came from a cookbook published in the 1930s. Her mother made them every Christmas for years, and now she's inherited the duty. Denise's caramels cannot be hurried. So set a stool by the stove, put on some relaxing music, arm yourself with a comfortable wooden spoon, and get ready to stir, and stir, and stir. It takes at least 1 hour of constant tending to get these irresistible candies to the proper temperature. Your patience will be rewarded by the end result: sweet, soft, vanilla-scented caramels that slowly melt on your tongue (provided you have the self-control to keep from chewing them). Although Denise finds it challenging to fit making these into her busy holiday schedule, she's always glad that she did. "If you make yourself take the time, it's very relaxing," she says. Make sure you have a candy thermometer handy before you begin.

Yield: About 5 dozen caramels

2 cups sugar

½ cup Lyle's Golden Syrup or light corn syrup

1 cup sweetened condensed milk

½ cup heavy whipping cream

1 cup whole milk

4 tablespoons salted butter

2 teaspoons vanilla extract

Grease a 9-inch square baking pan with butter or cooking spray. In a large, heavy saucepan, combine the sugar, corn syrup, condensed milk, cream, whole milk, and butter. Place over medium-high heat and stir until the mixture starts to bubble. Reduce the temperature to low and continue stirring, using a zigzag motion to ensure you are scraping all around the bottom of the pan. Stir constantly until the sugar mixture reaches the firm-ball stage (236°F) on a candy thermometer, about 1 hour and 15 minutes. (When done, the mixture will be a deep golden tan color.) Stir in the vanilla and pour the mixture into the prepared pan. Let the caramel stand until just cool enough to handle, about 15 minutes. Using a sharp, buttered knife, cut it into 1-inch squares. Wrap each caramel in a 4-inch square piece of waxed paper and twist each end to close. The caramels will keep for up to 4 days.

RATHER SWEET VARIATION

For nutty caramels, roll each caramel in chopped, toasted almonds, pecans, or walnuts.

Lola's Sunday Fudge

Lola Sale Bade is the ultimate elegant Southern woman. She lives in Victoria, Texas, in an impeccably decorated white-columned home, and her daughter, Lauren, who lives in Fredericksburg, is one of my closest friends. She gave me her mother's recipe when I reported that I was searching for great fudge to include in this book. I made the fudge and invited Lauren over to sample it. After taking one bite, silent tears spilled down her cheeks. She told me her mother used to make the treat every Sunday. It was one of her late father's favorites.

This is not your typical granular, fair-style fudge. It is a creamy, melt-in-your-mouth confection sure to capture any candy-loving heart. To wrap it, I use pinking shears to cut a sheet of waxed paper long enough to cover the bottom and sides of a square or rectangular cookie tin, plus enough of an overhang on two sides to cover the fudge once it has been placed in the tin.

Yield: About 16 pieces

1 cup whole milk

4 ounces high-quality unsweetened chocolate, such as Guittard or Ghirardelli, chopped

3 ounces 70 percent bittersweet chocolate, coarsely chopped

2 cups sugar

2 tablespoons light corn syrup

2 tablespoons unsalted butter

Pinch of kosher salt

1 teaspoon vanilla extract

Grease a 9-inch square baking pan with butter or cooking spray. In a medium saucepan, heat the milk over medium-high heat until it begins to steam. Add the chocolate, reduce the heat to low, and stir until the chocolate melts completely. Add the sugar and corn syrup. Continue cooking and slowly stirring until the sugar dissolves. Increase the heat to medium and bring to a boil. Cover and cook for 3 minutes. Uncover and cook, stirring frequently, until the mixture reaches the soft-ball stage, 234° to 240°F on a candy thermometer.

Remove from the heat and stir in the butter and salt. Let cool to warm, 110°F, without stirring. (This could take up to 30 minutes.) Add the vanilla and beat vigorously with a large spoon until the mixture is thick and is no longer glossy, about 5 minutes. Quickly spread in the prepared pan. Let cool for about 1 hour, then cut into squares.

Chocolate Sauce

Chocolate sauce is an ideal gift for a host of reasons: It keeps well (for at least 1 month in the refrigerator); it is versatile and can be used to top ice cream, pancakes, waffles, or fruit, or to flavor milkshakes; and almost everyone loves it. I use one master recipe to make chocolate sauce and supplement with extra ingredients to make additional flavors. If you wish, triple the basic recipe, then divide it into thirds and add different flavorings to each batch. To give as presents, pour a portion of each of the sauces into a clean jelly jar, stack them, and tie the group together with ribbons or raffia. (I also use invisible tape to hold them together and to give them extra stability.)

Yield: 1½ cups

1 cup heavy whipping cream

8 ounces bittersweet chocolate (I use El Rey's 70 percent bittersweet Venezuelan), chopped

2 tablespoons unsalted butter

¼ teaspoon kosher salt

1 tablespoon vanilla extract

In a medium saucepan, heat the cream and chocolate over medium-low heat, whisking constantly, until the chocolate is melted. Whisk in the butter until it melts completely. Remove from the heat and stir in the salt and vanilla. Pour into glass jars, cover, and refrigerate for up to 1 month.

RATHER SWEET VARIATIONS

To make Chocolate Malt Sauce, follow the recipe above. Whisk in ½ cup powdered instant malted milk with the butter.

To make Chocolate Cherry Sauce, follow the recipe above. Stir in ¼ cup kirsch (cherry liqueur) and ½ cup dried cherries or 1 cup halved and pitted fresh cherries with the salt and vanilla.

CHAPTER FIVE

NEW YEAR'S EVE

AS MUCH AS POSSIBLE, I try to stay off the roads on New Year's Eve. That means a one-destination itinerary, a little black dress, and a private party or a trip to one of my favorite nearby party spots. The Hill Top Café, located about ten miles north of Fredericksburg, is my favorite New Year's destination. Owned by Johnny and Brenda Nicholas, the restaurant features food that encompasses both their backgrounds: Cajun for her and Greek for him. Housed on the grounds of an old gas station that is complete with two nonfunctioning pumps near the entrance, it's always crowded, a little noisy, and full of good fun. Johnny can often be found stationed near the bar and seems to know just about everyone who comes through the door. As the evening wears on, if it's your lucky night he'll move to the piano in a corner of the dining room and sing a few tunes. A one-time member of the Texas swing band Asleep at the Wheel, Johnny still makes concert appearances with the Texas All Stars.

Last year, I went to an intimate private party at one of Fredericksburg's top restaurants, August E's, owned by Leu and Dawn Savanh. For a celebration of Chinese New Year, executive chef Leu Savanh started with a table full of specialties, including his signature Saigon spring rolls. At evening's end, Dawn gave every guest an envelope containing a personal New Year's wish, an idea worth emulating.

Dawn's thoughtful favors influenced me to create Good Luck Truffles (page 206), with twin purposes: The truffles provide a satisfying bittersweet bite-sized ending to a meal, and properly packaged, they can double as favors. Wrap them individually in squares of plastic wrap, write personalized New Year's wishes on strips of paper, place them half in and half out of the plastic wrapping, and fasten the packets with a silver or gold bow. Or, use similarly wrapped truffles as place cards by adding holiday tags with the guests' names written in metallic ink.

The New Year also lends itself to cozy celebrations at home, and the recipes in this chapter should give you enough ideas for several little dinner parties. I've learned that having a passed hors d'oeuvre such as thin-sliced Wild Mushroom and Goat Cheese Quesadillas (page 186) gives me a chance to greet guests with the warmest of welcomes—a savory bite to eat. Mother's Lobster Bisque (page 190) makes a rich first course that is surprisingly fast to make, and Caramel Pie with Meringue Topping (see page 203), provides enough pizzazz for a rousing celebration of the New Year.

Alice Lon's Champagne Punch

My mother's cousin, Alice Lon, was the first "Champagne Lady" on the nationally televised Laurence Welk Show in 1955. Alice sang and danced on the musical variety show in jewel-hued dresses with voluminous petticoats and nipped-in waistlines. She became a cause célèbre when Welk fired her on camera for crossing her legs on top of a desk, a move that was too racy for Welk's conservative sensibilities. Thousands of ABC viewers disagreed and sent an avalanche of mail to the network. Always sensitive to the views of his audience, Welk apologized and tried to rehire Alice, but she refused.

Before she left Welk's show, Alice's full petticoats attracted much attention from viewers. According to a 1956 TV Guide article, readers "wonder about the secret of the petticoats' fullness. What's more, Alice's mother, Mrs. Lois Wyche, of Kilgore, Tex., uses only nine yards of material to achieve the bouffant effect, turning out a petticoat on her sewing machine in about three hours."

{ Yield: 6 to 8 servings }

6 cups water

4 cups sugar

2 limes, scrubbed and sliced

2 tangerines, scrubbed and sliced

2 lemons, scrubbed and sliced

½ cup freshly squeezed orange juice

½ cup freshly squeezed lime juice

1 bottle brut sparkling wine or Champagne

½ cup Grand Marnier liqueur

12 to 14 kumquats, halved and frozen, for garnish (optional)

In a large saucepan, combine the water and sugar. Bring to a boil over medium-high heat and cook for 30 minutes, or until thickened. Add the sliced limes, tangerines, and lemons. Reduce the heat to medium and simmer for 30 minutes. Remove the syrup from the heat and let cool for 15 minutes. Transfer the syrup to a pitcher and stir in the orange and lime juice. Refrigerate until cold. (The syrup will keep in the refrigerator for about 1 week.)

To make individual cocktails, fill a Champagne flute half full with cold syrup and add Champagne until the glass is three-fourths full. Float 1 ounce of Grand Marnier on top.

RATHER SWEET VARIATION

To fill a punch bowl, pour 1 cup chilled syrup into a large punch bowl. Add the Champagne and the Grand Marnier. Stir until combined. Float frozen kumquats on top. Serve with a punch ladle.

Wild Mushroom and Goat Cheese Quesadillas with Cranberry-Pecan Salsa

We created an evening tapas bar at the café a few years ago as an experiment. Customers loved it, but it soon became obvious that it was too much of a strain for our staff. One of the most popular dishes was an open-faced wild mushroom quesadilla topped with greens. Recently, a longtime regular mentioned them with fondness, so I decided to resurrect them as an appetizer. I skipped the greens and came up with a cranberry salsa to give the dish some holiday flair. This easily made salsa adds such a welcome burst of flavor and complements the goat cheese so beautifully that I never serve my mushroom quesadillas without it.

{ Yield: 4 to 6 main-course servings or 24 appetizers }

SALSA

- ½ cup whole pecans
- 3 tablespoons balsamic vinegar
- 2 tablespoons olive oil
- ⅓ cup sugar
- 1 tablespoon Dijon mustard
- Grated zest and juice of 1 orange
- Kosher salt and freshly ground pepper to taste
- 2 cups fresh or thawed frozen cranberries
- 1 shallot, sliced
- 1 jalapeño pepper, seeded and minced (optional)

- ½ cup (1 stick) unsalted butter
- 1 yellow onion, coarsely chopped
- 1½ pounds mixed wild and commercial mushrooms, such as chanterelles, shiitakes, or oysters, sliced (shiitakes should be stemmed as well)
- 1 pound button or cremini mushrooms, sliced

- 4 cloves garlic, minced
- 1 teaspoon kosher salt
- 2 tablespoons Worcestershire sauce
- ⅔ cup dry white wine
- ½ teaspoon ground white pepper
- Eight 8-inch flour tortillas
- 2 cups (8 ounces) shredded Monterey jack cheese
- 3 cups (15 ounces) crumbled fresh goat cheese

To make the salsa: Preheat the oven to 350°F. Arrange the pecans on a rimmed baking sheet in a single layer and toast them in the oven for 7 to 9 minutes, until deeper brown and aromatic. Transfer to a bowl, let cool, and coarsely chop the pecans.

In a food processor, combine the vinegar, olive oil, sugar, mustard, orange zest, orange juice,

continued

salt, and pepper. Process until thoroughly combined, about 30 seconds. Make sure you combine the vinaigrette before adding the fruit. The mixture becomes cloudy and less attractive if you process all ingredients at once. Then again, if you don't, it will still taste as good.

Add the cranberries, shallot, and jalapeño and pulse until the cranberries are coarsely chopped. Pour the salsa into a medium bowl, cover, and refrigerate until ready to serve. Stir in the pecans just prior to serving.

In a large sauté pan, melt the butter over medium-high heat, add the onion and sauté for about 4 minutes, until translucent. Add the mushrooms, garlic, salt, and Worcestershire and sauté for about 5 minutes. Add the white wine and pepper and cook the mushrooms until the liquid is absorbed, at least 5 minutes.

While the mushrooms cook, coat a griddle or large skillet with cooking spray and heat over high heat, then reduce the heat to medium. Lay 2 tortillas on the griddle or in the skillet and cover each with ¼ cup of the Monterey jack. Evenly spread about ⅓ cup of the mushroom mixture on one half of each tortilla and cover the mushroom mixture evenly with a thin layer of crumbled goat cheese. Use a metal spatula to fold each tortilla in half and cook until lightly brown and crisp on the bottom. Flip and cook until brown on the other side. Transfer to a plate in a warm oven. Repeat with the remaining tortillas.

Cut each folded tortilla into 3 wedges and serve warm or at room temperature, with the salsa alongside.

♕ **TIP:** You may have leftover salsa. Refrigerate it for later use. It will keep for up to 3 weeks. It's a great accompaniment to Texas Spice-Rubbed Roast Pork (page 150) or Cajun Roast Turkey (page 154).

Paula's Scallop, Pancetta, and Radicchio Salad

A sensational New Year's Eve salad from girlfriend and fellow chef Paula Disbrowe, author of Cowgirl Cuisine: Rustic Recipes and Cowgirl Adventures from a Texas Ranch. She writes: "I love to serve this festive salad with champagne or a minerally white wine as the first course to a special meal. To get this salad just right, the salad needs to be well seasoned and the scallops need to be seared in a hot skillet so they get crispy and browned (but not overcooked)."

{ Yield: 4 first courses }

5 tablespoons extra-virgin olive oil

4 thin slices pancetta (about 2 ounces total)

2 tablespoons sherry wine vinegar

2 teaspoons Dijon mustard

2 tablespoons freshly squeezed lemon juice

Kosher salt and freshly ground pepper to taste

Leaves removed from 2 heads radicchio, thinly sliced

1 bunch radishes, thinly sliced

8 ounces bay scallops

In a large nonstick skillet, heat 1 tablespoon of the olive oil over medium-high heat and swirl to coat. Add the pancetta slices (in batches if necessary so as not to overcrowd the pan) and cook until crispy, about 2 minutes on each side. Transfer the cooked pancetta to a plate covered with paper towels to drain.

In a large bowl, whisk together 3 tablespoons of the olive oil, the vinegar, mustard, and lemon juice. Season with salt and pepper, then add the radicchio and radishes. Toss well to coat.

Heat the remaining 1 tablespoon olive oil over medium-high heat in the same skillet in which you cooked the pancetta. Generously season the scallops with salt and pepper and add to the skillet. Cook until crisp and brown on the first side, about 3 minutes, then turn and cook for about 2 minutes on the second side. Remove from the heat.

Divide the radicchio salad among 4 salad plates. Top each with seared scallops and a round of pancetta. Serve immediately.

Mother's Lobster Bisque

I adapted this recipe from one found in my mother's tiny white notebook—the one she used to write down recipes for a planned sodium-free cookbook for dialysis patients. She never finished the project, but the recipes have been a source of inspiration for me.

Cutting through the tough lobster shell to extract the meat is the most taxing part of this recipe. For that, you'll need a sharp knife and some muscle, but once it's done, the soup comes together very quickly. Make sure to buy lobster tails from a seafood purveyor you trust so that you can avoid additives such as sodium tripolyphosphate, which smothers the lobster meat's delicate, sweet flavor and makes it unduly salty.

{ Yield: 8 servings }

4 medium lobster tails (1 to 1½ pounds total)

2 teaspoons kosher salt

1 teaspoon cayenne pepper

½ cup (1 stick) unsalted butter

1 tablespoon finely chopped white onion or shallot

1 teaspoon garlic, minced

6 tablespoons all-purpose flour

5 cups milk

2 cups heavy whipping cream

1 tablespoon minced fresh flat-leaf parsley

2 tablespoons minced fresh chives

1 teaspoon ground white pepper

Pinch of hot Hungarian paprika

¼ cup freshly squeezed lemon juice

Place the lobster tails on a cutting board with the underside of the shell facing up. Using a sharp knife, pierce the shell at the top of the widest part and cut the tail (through both shell and meat) in half lengthwise. Turn the shell over, pull the meat out, and rub the meat all over with a mixture of 1 teaspoon of the salt and the cayenne pepper. Cut the meat into 1-inch slices.

In a large, heavy pot, melt the butter over medium heat. Add the onion and sauté until translucent but not browned, about 4 minutes. Stir in the garlic and sauté until fragrant, about 2 minutes. Whisk in the flour and cook, whisking constantly, for about 1 minute. Whisk in the milk, cream, and lobster. Reduce the heat to low and cook, whisking, until slightly thickened, 5 to 10 minutes. Stir in the remaining teaspoon of salt, the parsley, chives, pepper, paprika, and lemon juice. Do not boil. Serve immediately.

RATHER SWEET VARIATION

I love tarragon's strong, assertive flavor, so I add 1 tablespoon minced fresh tarragon or 1 teaspoon dried tarragon to the soup along with the paprika. Adding a tablespoon of Pernod, an anise-flavored liqueur, to each bowl of soup just before serving is another option.

Black-Eyed Peas with Bacon, Onions, and Garlic

I grew up on all kinds of peas: purple hull, black-eyed, cream. It's a Southern thing. We always had black-eyed peas for New Year's Day because they were supposed to be good luck. We ate peas all summer, too, and my mother would buy up a bunch of fresh ones and freeze them for wintertime. Just like her, I buy up extra in the summer and freeze them for holiday feasting. Fresh black-eyed peas may be difficult to find outside of the South, but you can use frozen or dried for this recipe.

Mom always added baking soda to her beans, but I never knew why. I recently asked my cousin, and she told me the soda makes peas and beans more tender.

{ Yield: 6 to 8 servings }

5 cups frozen shelled black-eyed peas, or 2 cups (1 pound) dried black-eyed peas

4 slices bacon (I prefer apple smoked), chopped

1 yellow onion, chopped

2 stalks celery, diced

1 red bell pepper, seeded, deveined, and diced

1 green bell pepper, seeded, deveined, and diced

1 jalapeño pepper, seeded and minced

4 cloves garlic, minced

5 to 6 cups water or chicken stock

2 teaspoons kosher salt

2 dashes Tabasco sauce

1 teaspoon baking soda

¼ cup chopped green onion tops

1 teaspoon white wine vinegar

If using frozen black-eyed peas, put them in a colander and run warm water over them for a few minutes. (This will separate them; it is not necessary to defrost them fully.) For dried peas, follow the package directions for soaking, then drain and cook as directed below.

In a large, heavy pot, fry the bacon over medium-high heat for 3 to 4 minutes, until cooked but not crisp. Add the onion, celery, bell peppers, jalapeño, and garlic. Reduce the heat to medium and sauté until the vegetables are soft but not browned, about 5 minutes. Add the water or stock, salt, Tabasco, peas, and baking soda. Increase the heat to high and bring to a boil. Reduce the heat to a simmer and cook uncovered until the beans are tender, about 1 hour. Stir in the green onion tops and vinegar. Serve immediately, or let cool and refrigerate for up to 3 days. Reheat to serve.

Shrimp 'n' Grits

I recently asked a well-known restaurateur in Charleston, South Carolina, for the secret to creamy grits. "Lots of cream and butter," she said, in her luscious Southern drawl. What prompted the question? A fabulous rendition of the Southern specialty, shrimp and grits, that I tasted on Pawleys Island. I traveled there for the wedding of my friend and fellow chef Paula Disbrowe to David Norman. It was truly a foodie wedding; we feasted on the indigenous cuisine that is a veritable stew of influences, from African and Caribbean to European and American. When I returned home, I headed to the kitchen and came up with my own version of shrimp and grits—comfort food at its most soul-satisfying best. Although it takes time, it's worth it to make a stock from the shrimp shells. If time is short, substitute commercial seafood stock and buy uncooked shrimp already shelled and deveined.

{ **Yield: 6 servings** }

GRITS

3 cups milk

2 cups half-and-half

½ teaspoon kosher salt

1 cup quick white grits

½ cup (1 stick) unsalted butter

1 cup grated Parmesan cheese

SHRIMP

1½ teaspoons kosher salt

2 teaspoons Cajun seasoning

24 large (16 to 20 count) fresh or frozen shrimp, shelled and deveined (reserve shells for stock)

6 slices bacon

1 onion, diced

1 green bell pepper, seeded, deveined, and diced

2 stalks celery, diced

3 cloves garlic, minced

1 cup cremini or mixed wild and commercial mushrooms

¼ cup all-purpose flour

4 cups shrimp stock (recipe follows) or commercial fish stock

Juice of ½ lemon

Dash of Tabasco or Crystal hot sauce

½ teaspoon freshly ground pepper

To make the grits: In a large saucepan, heat the milk, half-and-half, and salt over medium-high heat until it steams. Gradually stir in the grits and cook, stirring occasionally, for about 10 minutes. Stir in the butter and Parmesan until completely melted. The grits should be creamy and loose, like cream of wheat. If they seem too thick, add water.

To make the shrimp: In a small bowl, mix together 1 teaspoon of the salt and the Cajun seasoning. Rub the mixture all over the shrimp. Place in a medium bowl, cover, and refrigerate.

In a large, heavy pot, fry the bacon over medium-high heat until crisp. Using tongs,

continued

transfer to paper towels to drain; reserve for another use. Add the onion, bell pepper, celery, and garlic to the bacon fat in the pot and cook over medium heat until tender, about 5 minutes. Add the mushrooms and cook another 5 minutes, until the mushrooms have given up their juice and reabsorbed it again. Sprinkle the flour over the vegetables and cook, stirring, until it is absorbed. Gradually whisk in the stock and cook, whisking constantly, until thickened and creamy. Stir in the lemon juice, hot sauce, the remaining ½ teaspoon salt, and the pepper. Add the shrimp and simmer, stirring occasionally, for 3 to 4 minutes, until they turn pink.

To serve: Spoon grits into 6 soup bowls and divide the shrimp mixture among them. Eat immediately.

Shrimp Stock

{ Yield: About 4 cups }

2 tablespoons olive oil

1 unpeeled onion, cut into 6 pieces

1 large carrot, cut into 4 pieces

2 stalks celery, cut into 8 pieces

2 cloves garlic, peeled

1 slice bacon

Shells from 24 large shrimp

2 tablespoons tomato paste

2 cups dry white wine

4 cups water

½ teaspoon kosher salt

In a large stockpot, heat the olive oil over medium-high heat. Add the onion, carrot, celery, garlic, and bacon and sauté until the vegetables are tender, 8 to 10 minutes. Add the shrimp shells and sauté until they turn

light brown, about 5 minutes. Stir in the tomato paste, wine, water, and salt. Bring to a boil, reduce the heat to medium-low, and simmer for 1 hour. Strain the stock into a large container. The stock can be made 1 day in advance, cooled, covered, and refrigerated.

TIP: Ball's Cajun Seasoning is a special, spicy blend developed at a fried-chicken shack in Louisiana. To order, call 337-436-0291 for more information.

RATHER SWEET VARIATION

Stone-ground grits can be hard to find outside of the South. They take longer to cook than their regular counterparts, but their flavor and superior texture easily makes up for it. Substitute them for quick grits in this recipe and follow package directions for cooking times. For mail-order grits, try Anson Mills at www.ansonmills.com or Charleston Favorites at www.charlestonfavorites.com.

Ken Hall's Standing Rib Roast

Known as "the Sugar Land Express," former running back Ken Hall still holds several national high-school records, even though it's been more than fifty years since he graduated from Sugar Land (Texas) High. But the numbers that mean the most to the former pro ball player (his five-year career ended when he broke his back during an exhibition game as a Baltimore Colt) have nothing to do with sports. He's mentored sixty-six high-school kids, all of whom worked for him during an eighteen-year stint as owner, with wife Gloria, of Ken Hall's Barbecue Place in Fredericksburg.

"The best part came from reaching out to young people," Ken says. Hall gave his young employees more than a weekly pay check. He worked with each one to teach them the rudiments of successful living: how to work hard, accept responsibility, weather rejection, and get along with others in a work setting. More than a few of his former employees credit Ken's special brand of tough love with turning their lives around.

Ken sold the barbecue business to retire in 2003, but his passion for cooking continues. He and Gloria, high-school sweethearts who have been happily married for more than fifty years, love to entertain family and friends during the holidays. Standing rib roast is one of Ken's specialties. Searing the meat in a hot skillet before roasting is the key to great taste, Ken says. He also suggests that if one of your guests requests well-done prime rib, "don't invite them back."

{ Yield: 8 to 12 servings }

One 8-pound 4-bone prime rib of beef, choice grade

¼ cup olive oil

1½ tablespoons kosher salt

1 tablespoon freshly ground black pepper (medium grind)

Leaves from 6 thyme sprigs, minced

Ask your butcher to slice between the bones and meat, and then tie the bones back into place for roasting and easy carving. Place the roast on a large cutting board and let stand at room temperature for about 1 hour. Lightly coat the meat with olive oil. Evenly pat the salt, pepper, and thyme into the roast. Let the roast rest for an additional 30 minutes. If some of the seasoning has fallen off, roll the roast in any that has collected on the cutting board.

Preheat the oven to 425°F. Heat a large, heavy skillet or roasting pan over medium-high heat and sear the meat on all sides, including the bones, 7 to 8 minutes total. Transfer to the oven and roast for 25 minutes, then reduce the oven temperature to 250°F and continue roasting until a meat thermometer placed

continued

in the center of the meatiest portion of the roast (not touching bone) reads 115°F for rare, 125°F for medium-rare, and 130°F for medium. (Once the oven temperature is reduced, it will take about 2 more hours for medium, less for rare or medium-rare.) Remove from the oven and let rest for 30 minutes before carving. The meat will continue to cook after being taken from the oven. Resting also "gives the wonderful juices time to slow down their haste and keeps them from wandering around on your cutting board not being enjoyed," Ken says.

Save the end slices for those who like their meat better done. Carve and serve the meat on warmed dinner plates.

No-Peeking Popovers

Popovers have been around forever, but I fell in love with them all over again at a wonderful dinner at New York City's BLT Steak. They were brought to the table huge and warm, straight from the oven—by far the best and, as far as I am concerned, the only way to serve them. When I returned home, I began popover research. Most everyone uses essentially the same recipe. After much experimentation, I came up with two ironclad rules for success: (1) Never open the oven to peek before the popovers are done. This leads to popover flop. (2) Make sure to use a hot oven, which ensures the highest popover possible. I also found that unbleached high-protein flour (such as King Arthur's) works best. But don't stress too much over this; they'll work fine no matter what flour you use. It all comes down to this: What is better than a warm, melt-in-your-mouth popover on a cold night? Try them as an accompaniment to Ken Hall's Standing Rib Roast (page 195).

{ Yield: 6 large popovers }

6 teaspoons unsalted butter

3 large eggs at room temperature

1½ cups whole milk at room temperature

1½ cups unbleached all-purpose flour

½ teaspoon kosher salt

1 tablespoon unsalted butter, melted

6 tablespoons grated cheese, such as
   Gruyère, sharp Cheddar, or Parmesan

Preheat the oven to 425°F. Use a cast-iron popover pan, which has especially deep cups, or a Texas-sized muffin pan (with 3¾-inch cups) for this recipe. Each has 6 cups. Put 1 teaspoon butter in each popover or muffin cup and set aside. In a large bowl, whisk together the eggs and milk until combined. Whisk in the flour, salt, and melted butter.

Place the pan in the oven until the butter melts, about 2 minutes. Remove the pan from the oven and fill each cup half full with batter. Top the batter in each cup with 1 tablespoon of cheese. Pour in the rest of the batter until each cup is three-fourths full. Return the pan to the oven and increase the oven temperature to 450°F. Bake for 15 minutes, then reduce temperature to 350°F and bake for 15 minutes more. Resist the temptation to open the oven door until baking is complete. Remove the popovers from the oven and immediately invert the pan to remove them. Don't be slow, or the popovers may stick. Serve immediately.

RATHER SWEET VARIATION

Artisan salt lovers can experiment by topping each muffin with a sprinkling of their favorite salt just after the popovers emerge from the oven. My current favorite is Himalayan sea salt, a fine-textured pink salt.

TIP: Do not try to make popovers using egg substitute. They will not pop.

Glazed Chocolate Pavé

Here's an elegant plated dessert that will top off your holiday dinner with a grand flourish. I used to make a similar dessert when I worked as a pastry chef for Houston restaurateur Tony Vallone. It's a wickedly rich and dense dessert made with fine chocolate, butter, cream, and egg yolks, which I made in a loaf pan, slicing it thin and serving it with a custard sauce.

For the home cook, I think individual desserts provide more drama. And what harried holiday cook needs the extra work of making custard sauce? You can do much of the work several days in advance, but to preserve the dessert's arresting chocolate sheen, glazing must be done within several hours of serving. To make the dessert party-worthy, I decorate the pavés with broken chocolate bars that have been painted gold or silver with a special colored powder called Luster Dust (to order Luster Dust, call 800-776-0575 or visit the website at www.kitchencrafts.com).

{ Yield: 6 individual desserts }

8 ounces bittersweet chocolate (70 percent cacao), chopped

4 tablespoons unsalted butter

3 large egg yolks

Pinch of kosher salt

2 tablespoons good-quality unsweetened cocoa powder

½ cup heavy whipping cream

GLAZE

12 ounces bittersweet chocolate (70 percent cacao), chopped

1 cup heavy whipping cream, plus extra for thinning if needed

½ cup Lyle's Golden syrup or light corn syrup

Pinch of kosher salt

One 4-ounce bar bittersweet chocolate, such as Ghirardelli

Gold or silver Luster Dust for decorating

1 teaspoon brandy or liqueur such as Grand Marnier or Amaretto

Evenly coat six 2½-inch (about ⅓-cup capacity) molds or ramekins with cooking spray. In a medium saucepan, bring 1 inch of water to a simmer over medium-low heat. In a large stainless-steel bowl, combine the chocolate and butter. Place on top of the saucepan and melt completely. Whisk in the egg yolks and salt until combined. Remove the bowl from the pan, sprinkle the cocoa powder evenly over the chocolate mixture, and whisk until combined. Set aside.

Using an electric mixer fitted with the whisk attachment, beat the cream until soft peaks form. Using a large rubber spatula, fold the whipped cream into the chocolate mixture. Keep folding until no white is showing and the mixture is smooth and silky. Spoon the chocolate mixture evenly into the ramekins. Refrigerate, uncovered, for at least 2 hours; cover with plastic wrap if keeping up to 3 days.

continued

To make the glaze: Put the chocolate in a large bowl. In a small saucepan, heat the cream over medium heat until steaming but not boiling. Pour the hot cream over the chocolate and stir until it has melted completely. Stir in the syrup and salt. Let the glaze cool for about 10 minutes.

To assemble the pavé: While the glaze is setting, unmold the pavés. Working with one at a time, dip each chocolate-filled ramekin for a few seconds in hot water that reaches just below the top rim. Be careful not to get any water on the chocolate. Unmold each ramekin onto a dessert plate. The chocolate should slide out easily. If not, dip it in hot water for a second or two more.

The glaze should now be pourable. If it is too thick, add a little cream, 1 tablespoon at a time. Spoon enough glaze over each pavé to cover and surround it with a small puddle. Using a small metal spatula, smooth the glaze on the top and sides. Let the glaze set for at least 30 minutes before serving or decorating.

To decorate, break the chocolate bar into ½- to 1-inch pieces. Do not cut it neatly; you want a jagged look. In a small bowl, mix ¼ teaspoon Luster Dust with a few drops of the brandy or liqueur. (Luster Dust is not water soluble.) Using a small, clean paintbrush, paint designs of your choice on the chocolate bar pieces. Arrange them vertically by pressing them gently into the middle of the top of the pavé. (Think Stonehenge.)

Frances's Bread and Jam Pudding

I named this dessert after my daughter Frances's favorite children's book, Bread and Jam for Frances by Russell Hoban. She loved the book, about a badger named Frances, and she loved my bread pudding, which became a Christmas tradition. Nothing beats bread pudding made with challah, the traditional Jewish egg bread. Check with your local grocery store about the availability of challah. Traditionally eaten on the Jewish Sabbath, some stores order it to have on hand toward the end of the week.

{ Yield: 10 to 12 servings }

1 loaf challah bread
1 large egg
4 large egg yolks
1 cup sugar
1 vanilla bean, split lengthwise
2 cups heavy whipping cream

¼ cup high-quality raspberry jam
¼ cup high-quality apricot jam

Place the oven rack in the center of the oven and preheat the oven to 300°F. Line a standard loaf pan with parchment paper, leaving generous flaps hanging over the long sides of the pan. Use a serrated knife to cut the crusts off the bread. (No need to be precise; the pudding looks best with bits of dark brown crust showing.) Cut the loaf in 3 even lengthwise slices. In a large bowl, whisk together the egg, egg yolks, and sugar. In a medium saucepan, combine the vanilla bean and cream and bring to a boil over medium-high heat. Remove the pan from the heat as soon as the cream begins to bubble and rise up the sides of the pan, taking care not to let it boil over. Remove the vanilla bean. Using the tip of a thin-bladed knife, scrape the tiny seeds out of the center of each vanilla bean half. Stir the vanilla seeds into the cream. Whisk about one-fourth of the hot cream into the egg mixture. (This tempers the egg and prevents it from scrambling.) Gradually whisk in the remaining cream until combined. Place a slice of challah bread in the bottom of the prepared pan. Pour in one-third of the cream mixture to cover. Press the challah lightly with the back of a large spoon and let it sit for about 1 minute so the cream can soak into the bread. Spoon a line of raspberry jam down the center of the soaked bread. Add the second slice of challah on top and soak with one-third of the cream mixture. Spoon a line of apricot jam down the center of the second slice. Top with the remaining challah slice and cream mixture.

Place the loaf pan in a larger baking pan and place it on the middle rack of the oven. Use a teakettle to pour enough boiling water into the baking pan to reach halfway up the sides of the loaf pan. Bake for about 1 hour, or until lightly browned and crisp, with no wet spots. Remove from the oven and let cool on a wire rack for at least 1 hour. Use the parchment paper handles to lift the bread pudding out of the pan. Peel the parchment from the sides of the pudding, slice, and serve warm or at room temperature.

RATHER SWEET VARIATION

Leftover bread pudding makes wonderful French toast. In a large skillet, melt 1 tablespoon butter over medium heat, and fry the slices until golden brown and crisp, about 2 minutes on each side. (Add more butter as needed to fry more than 1 batch.) Serve with butter, warm maple syrup, or fruit sauce.

TIP: Raspberry and apricot jams are my favorites for this recipe, but any good-quality jam will work.

Caramel Pie with Meringue Topping

Our Wright family reunion takes place every June in a tree-shaded Elderville churchyard in East Texas. First, we attend services in the quaint little white church, then we walk through the old, gated cemetery to pay our respects. (My maternal grandparents, great-grandparents, and other relatives are buried there. Numerous living relatives already have their plots staked out, and I'd be fibbing if I claimed there'd never been a skirmish over prospective resting places.) After a walk through the cemetery, we all meet in the churchyard for dinner on the grounds. Everyone totes a picnic basket filled with some family favorite. Uncle Roger Glenn brings his famous brined fried chicken. Great-Aunt Mary Harrell is gone, but her fabulous caramel pie continues to make an annual appearance, and an equally fast disappearance. (It's that good.) For years, my cousin Vera tried to finagle the recipe from my Aunt Mary. Aunt Mary would hem and haw and say she'd get it to her. Nothing happened. Vera finally appealed to my Aunt Mary Lois. "I'll get it," Mary Lois said with confidence. Again, no luck. Finally, inexplicably, Aunt Mary gave it to one of her daughters-in-law. I tasted it again at a recent family reunion and begged for the recipe. I got it, but the directions were scant. My friend Sam and I spent an evening in my kitchen working out the directions. We used her favorite sour-cream-kissed piecrust recipe, which she adapted from an old magazine article. I topped the pie with my signature meringue crown, and the result is as dramatic as it is delicious. You'll need a 10-inch deep-dish pie plate to make this pie.

{ Yield: 8 to 10 servings }

CRUST

- 2½ cups all-purpose flour
- 1 teaspoon kosher salt
- 1 tablespoon sugar
- 1 cup (2 sticks) cold unsalted butter, cut into ½-inch cubes and frozen for 10 minutes
- 3 tablespoons sour cream
- ⅓ cup ice water

CUSTARD

- 3½ cups milk
- 2½ cups sugar
- 6 large egg yolks, lightly beaten
- 4 heaping tablespoons all-purpose flour
- 4 tablespoons unsalted butter
- 12 large marshmallows
- 2 teaspoons vanilla extract

TOPPING

- 10 extra-large egg whites at room temperature
- 3 cups sugar

continued

To make the crust: Preheat the oven to 450°F. In a food processor, combine the flour, salt, and sugar and process for 3 seconds. Add the butter and pulse until the mixture looks crumbly, with bits of dough the size of small grapes. In a small bowl, mix the sour cream and ice water together. Add the sour cream mixture to the flour mixture and give it three 1-second pulses. On a floured work surface, form the dough into a ball and divide in half. Gently mold the dough into 2 disks, cover each in plastic wrap, and refrigerate for at least 2 hours. (The second crust can be refrigerated for up to 1 week or frozen for up to 1 month.)

Roll the dough out to a ⅛-inch thickness on a generously floured work surface. Fold it over the rolling pin and gently transfer the dough to a 10-inch, deep-dish pie plate. Press it lightly into place, cut off any excess dough that falls over the edge of the pie plate, and crimp the edges with a fork. Line the crust with parchment paper or aluminum foil, fill it with dried beans or pie weights, and bake for 10 minutes, or until the crust turns a light golden brown. Remove from the oven, remove the paper or foil, and let the piecrust cool on a wire rack for at least 30 minutes before filling.

To make the custard: In an 8-cup saucepan, whisk the milk and 1½ cups of the sugar together over low heat. Whisk in the egg yolks and flour and continue to heat while you make the caramel. Keep an eye on the milk mixture; do not let it boil. In a large, heavy saucepan, cook the remaining 1 cup sugar over medium heat, stirring often until it melts and turns a deep golden brown, 20 to 25 minutes. Gradually pour the warmed milk mixture into the caramelized sugar and stir until smooth. (Watch out for spattering.) Add the butter, marshmallows, and vanilla.

Stir until the butter and marshmallows are melted, then pour into the prepared piecrust. Let cool, then refrigerate the pie while making the meringue topping.

To make the topping: Position an oven rack in the center of the oven. Preheat the broiler. In a large, clean stainless-steel bowl, combine the egg whites and sugar. (Warning: if there is even a trace of fat in the bowl, the eggs won't reach their proper volume.) Set the bowl over a saucepan with 2 inches of barely simmering water. Whisking constantly, heat the mixture until the sugar melts and there are no visible grains in the meringue. Rub a little bit of meringue between your fingers to make sure all the sugar grains have melted. Remove from the heat and beat using an electric mixer on low speed for 5 minutes; increase the speed to high and beat 5 minutes longer, or until the meringue is stiff and shiny.

Pile the meringue on top of the caramel custard. Style the meringue with your fingers or a spoon by plucking at it to tease the meringue into high, jagged spikes. Place the pie on the middle rack of the oven and broil until the meringue topping turns golden brown, about 1 minute. Watch the pie closely, as it can turn from browned to burned in a matter of seconds. If using a kitchen torch, hold it 2 to 3 inches away from the meringue and move the flame slowly around the meringue until it is browned all over. The pie should be served the day it is assembled.

♛ **TIP:** Sam's grandmother taught her to crimp a piecrust's edges by making a dent in the dough with her index finger knuckle and then placing her other hand's thumb and index finger on either side to crimp around her knuckle. It must be a Southern thing, because that's how I learned to do it, too.

Good Luck Truffles

This year I helped raise funds for Share Our Strength (SOS), a wonderful nonprofit created to end childhood hunger in America. The owners of Patrón, a Mexico-based tequila distiller and producer, asked me to come up with a dessert for an SOS benefit using their new café liqueur. I made mini s'mores bars and used the liqueur in a chocolate sauce that covered the bars. More than three hundred of them disappeared at an SOS event in just a few hours—one woman came back for seconds and thirds. The next day, I began thinking that a touch of liqueur would make a great filling for a chocolate truffle, and my Good Luck Truffles were born. I love serving a tray of truffles with coffee or espresso after a holiday dinner.

{ Yield: About 4 dozen truffles }

FILLING

1 cup heavy whipping cream

13 to 14 ounces bittersweet chocolate (I use El Rey's 70 percent cacao Gran Samán Bittersweet), chopped

3 tablespoons Patrón XO Cafe (tequila-coffee liqueur) or other coffee-flavored liqueur

2 tablespoons unsalted butter at room temperature

COATING

10 ounces bittersweet chocolate (at least 70 percent cacao), chopped

¾ cup unsweetened cocoa powder

To make the filling: In a medium saucepan, bring the cream to a low simmer over medium heat. Do not let it boil. Put the chocolate in a large bowl and pour the hot cream over it. Let stand for 5 minutes. Gently whisk the mixture, starting in the center of the bowl and slowly moving outward, until the cream is incorporated and the mixture is smooth. Whisk in the coffee liqueur. Let stand at room temperature for 2 to 4 hours until firm enough to scoop.

Fold in the butter with a large spatula until thoroughly blended.

Using a 1-inch ice cream scoop with a quick-release lever, scoop out balls to form the centers. (To create uniform centers with rounded tops and flat bottoms, fill the scoop with chocolate and use a straight knife or your finger to sweep off the excess chocolate on top.) Place the centers on a baking sheet lined with a waxed or parchment paper or a silicone liner. Refrigerate the centers until they harden, 15 to 30 minutes.

To make the coating: Put the chocolate in a medium stainless-steel bowl set over a saucepan with 2 inches of simmering water. Stir until melted and smooth. Remove the bowl from the pan and let cool until the bottom of the bowl is cool to the touch, about 30 minutes. (You can speed up the process by refrigerating the chocolate for about 10 to 15 minutes, but watch carefully to ensure it doesn't become too thick and hard for dipping.)

Sift the cocoa into a medium bowl for coating the truffles. Using a fork or a toothpick, spear the flat bottom of each truffle center and swirl it in the melted chocolate. Hold the truffle over the bowl, allowing the excess chocolate coating to drip back into the bowl. Return the dipped truffles to the lined baking sheet. Continue dipping until all of the truffles are coated. When the coating loses its glossy appearance (5 to 15 minutes, depending on the heat of the coating), roll each truffle in the bowl of cocoa to coat. The truffles can be refrigerated in an airtight container for up to 1 week. Let them come to room temperature for at least 1 hour before serving.

RATHER SWEET VARIATION

Chocolate-dipped truffles also can be rolled in finely chopped toasted nuts—almonds, walnuts, pecans, or hazelnuts—or in chocolate sprinkles. I prefer organic or natural sprinkles, which have a more pronounced chocolate flavor and are free of hydrogenated oils. Truffles should be rolled in nuts and sprinkles immediately after dipping them.

Appendix

GINGERBREAD HOUSE TEMPLATES

ENLARGE EACH PIECE AT 150%

Front and back walls

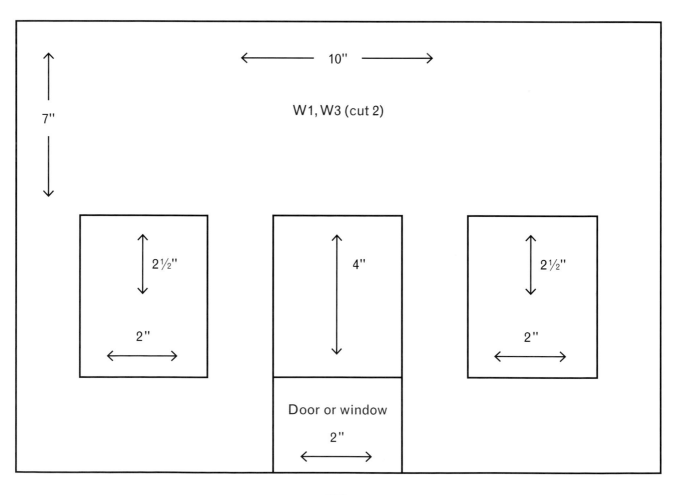

Side walls

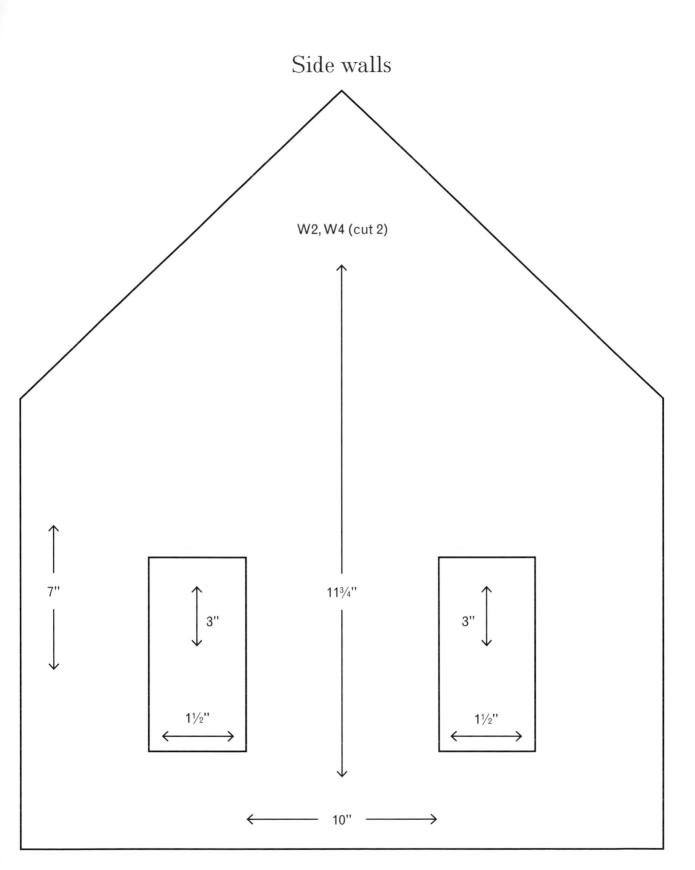

W2, W4 (cut 2)

11¾"

7"

3"

3"

1½"

1½"

10"

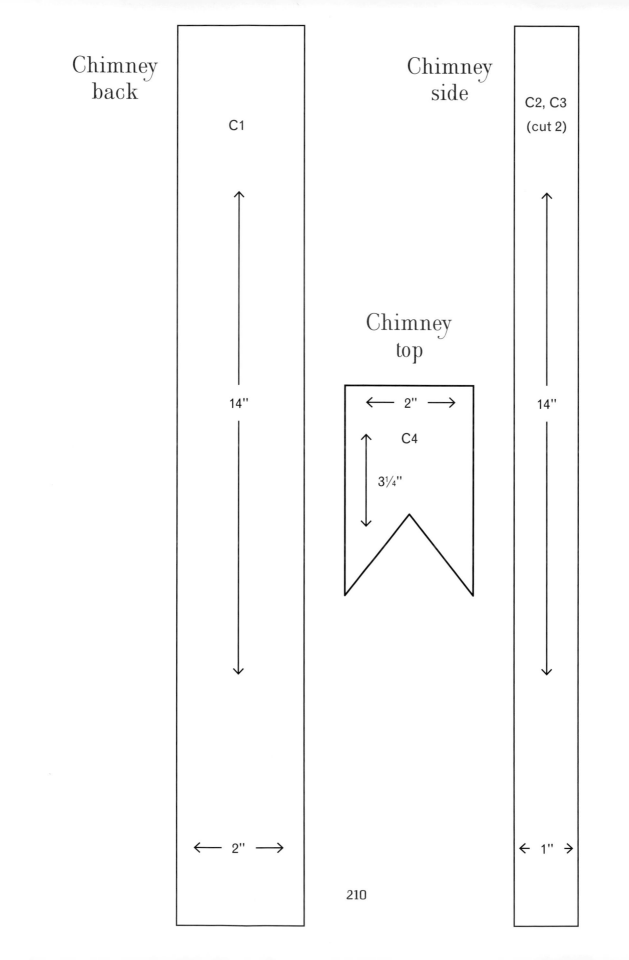

Chimney
back

C1

14"

2"

Chimney
side

C2, C3
(cut 2)

14"

1"

Chimney
top

2"

C4

3¼"

Eaves

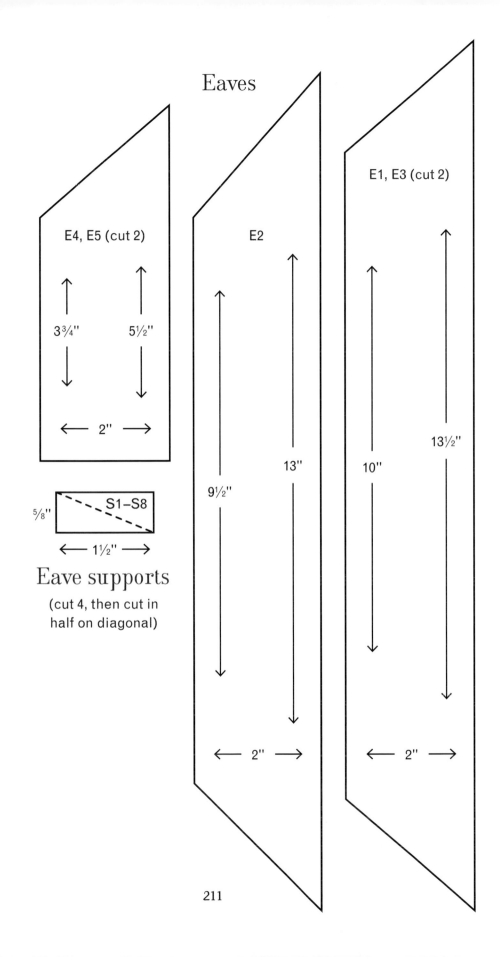

E4, E5 (cut 2)

3¾"   5½"

← 2" →

E2

9½"   13"

← 2" →

E1, E3 (cut 2)

10"   13½"

← 2" →

⅝" S1–S8

← 1½" →

Eave supports

(cut 4, then cut in
half on diagonal)

211

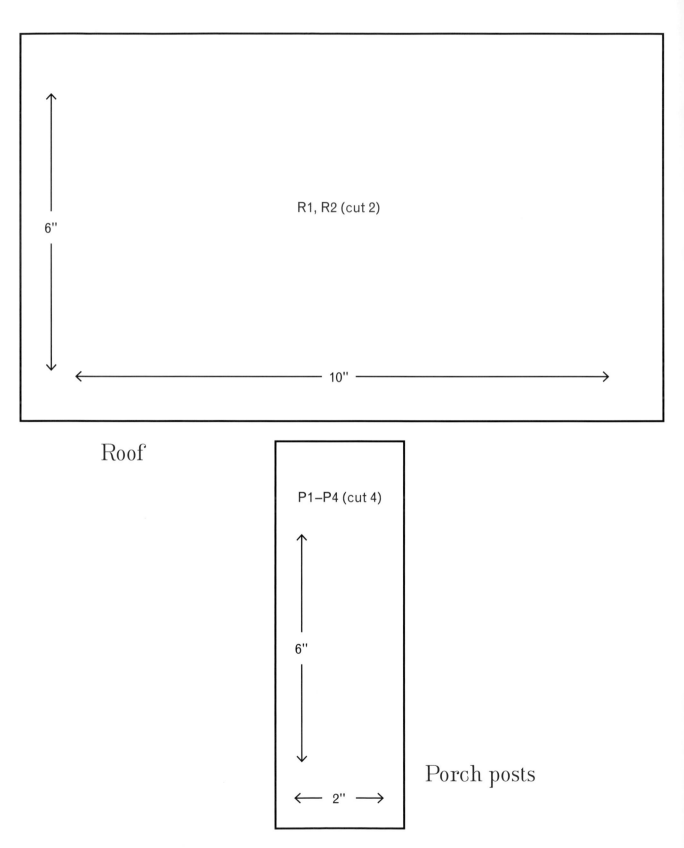

R1, R2 (cut 2)

6"

10"

Roof

P1–P4 (cut 4)

6"

2"

Porch posts

212

Cabin base

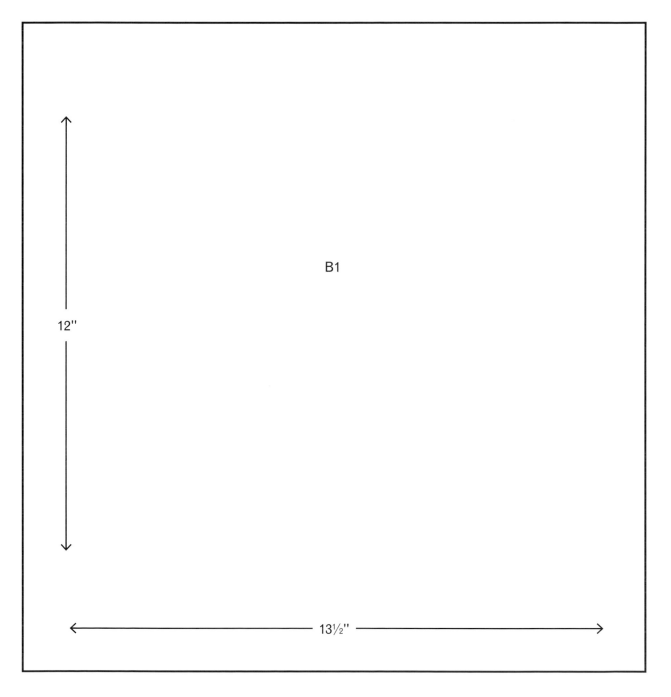

B1

12"

13½"

Index